# Ancestors
*Discover your*

# Discover Your Ancestors Periodical Compendium

## Volume I (May-Dec 2013)

### Edited by Andrew Chapman

**Discover Your Ancestors
Periodical Compendium**

First published in 2015
Discover Your Ancestors Publishing
www.discoveryourancestors.co.uk

Printed and bound in Great Britain by Acorn Web Offset, Wakefield

ISBN 978-1-911166-03-0

Edited by Andrew Chapman

Authors: Sharon Brookshaw, Andrew Chapman, Nell Darby,
Beryl Evans, Simon Fowler, Kirsty Gray, Emma Jolly, Mairead Mahon,
Paul Matthews, Jill Morris, David Osborne, Chris Paton, Dominic Rowe,
Jayne Shrimpton, Sue Wilkes

Design: Prepare to Publish Ltd

Note:
These articles were first published in the digital-only
*Discover Your Ancestors Periodical* between May and December 2013.
To subscribe, please visit **www.discoveryourancestors.co.uk**

# Contents

## Those magnificent men 5

The first British pilots' certificates were awarded just over a century ago – here we pay tribute to the pioneers of aviation

## Back to paper 8

Simon Fowler explains how to find records that aren't available online yet... and the internet can still help the process

## Suffer the little children? 11

For centuries, child labour was a reality for our ancestors. Sharon Brookshaw explores how a childhood of play is very much a modern invention

## Joining the dots 16

Powerful tools online can help you link birth, marriage and death records – and the censuses – together

## Voting for action 21

Only a century ago, women were starving themselves and worse just to get the vote. Nell Darby tells the story of the suffragettes

## Operation Chastise 26

Records of the famous Dam Busters raids are available online

## Church or chapel? 28

Worship has profoundly influenced Wales for centuries. Beryl Evans explores how to track down ancestors in both Nonconformist and Anglican communities

## The plot thickens 32

A pictorial guide to how surname and other distribution maps can provide useful clues on where your ancestors came from and where they may have gone next

## Thinking outside the pox 34

Every family would have been affected by smallpox. Sue Wilkes explores the history of vaccination and the marks it left in the archives

## Get your research on track 38

From the mid-19th century onwards the railways employed many people in a wide variety of roles – many of their work records are going online

## Far from home 40

Were your forebears among the British Home Children sent abroad? Emma Jolly explains how to trace them

## Lucky dip 44

A large and eclectic collection of name-based data has gone online – is your ancestor in there?

## Find ships' crews online 46

If you have ancestors who set sail with the Navy or merchant fleets in the 19th century, an online resource could help you

## Something for everyone 49

Mairead Mahon explores the history of department stores

## School records 53

Kirsty Gray offers an education in exploring our ancestors' childhoods through records from schooldays

## Lost way of life 56

Nell Darby explores a forgotten corner of London's history

## Light industry 60

Picture historian Jayne Shrimpton puts the lives of photographer ancestors in focus and explains and how to trace them

## Round up the black sheep 65

A selection of criminal register records available online may help shed light on a family relative who broke the law and paid the consequences...

### Forced from home 69

Scotland will never forget the brutal evictions of its crofters from the Highlands and islands. Chris Paton explores their legacy and how to trace Scots ancestors who migrated within the country or abroad

### Brought to court 72

Nell Darby explores the historic court system, starting with the Quarter Sessions

### Petty crimes? 76

Nell Darby looks at Petty Sessions

### The flying judges 79

Nell Darby concludes her series on the historic tiers of the court system with a look at the Assizes, which saw presiding judges travelling around the country

### Trade secrets 82

Apprenticeships have been a key part of many of our forebears' lives. Many apprenticeship records are available online

### The family killer 85

Paul Matthews explores how typhus ravaged many of our ancestors' lives through a sad example from his own research

### The skill of search 88

Here are some tips to get the most out of the unique Master Search features at TheGenealogist

### The back-up brigades 90

Did you have an ancestor who was a part-time soldier in the late 18th Century? Militia muster records online could help you advance your research

### Grande dame of the seas 94

The SS Great Britain took thousands of people to new lives in America and Australia – here we explore the archives of her distinguished career

### Know your place 97

Researching local history is a key skill for family historians and is a rewarding activity in its own right, as Jill Morris explains

### Picturing the past 102

Introducing a valuable online resource for bring the past to life

### Jutland remembered 104

Records from the largest naval battle of WW1 are online

# Those magnificent men

*The first British pilots' certificates were awarded just over a century ago – here we pay tribute to the pioneers of aviation*

British aviation began in the Edwardian era as a pastime of wealthy gentlemen. The first flight was conducted on 2 May 1909 at a country estate, now called Muswell Manor, on the Isle of Sheppey. This was the site of the first aerodrome in the country, set up by the Aero Club, which itself had begun in 1901 as a recreational ballooning society.

That first flight was taken by John Moore-Brabazon, who had become interested in flight through working for Charles Rolls, co-founder of Rolls-Royce and also the Aero Club itself. Brabazon, as with many other pioneers, learned to fly in France, and the club was keen to put England on the flight map, as it were. On 8 March 1910, Moore-Brabazon became the first person to qualify as a pilot in the UK and was awarded Aviator's Certificate number 1 by what had now been renamed the Royal Aero Club – his car even bore the numberplate FLY 1.

The early years of flight were marked by disasters as much as triumph, however, and only four months later, Charles Rolls was killed in a flying accident and Moore-Brabazon's wife persuaded him to give up flying.

The early records of the Royal Aero Club have been digitised by data

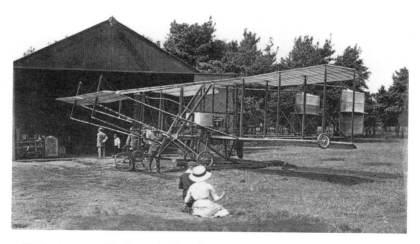

**The biplane used by Samuel F Cody in an early prize-winning tour of Britain**

# THE GREAT SHOWMAN

One of the first 10 people to be granted a flying certificate from the Royal Aero Club was Samuel F Cody. The new collection of pilots' records at **www.thegenealogist.co.uk** reveals a wealth of details about his life.

The records can be found under the Occupations section of the main search page – choose the Pilots option. We can now look up Cody simply by putting in his surname.

| Certifi-cate No. | Name. | Date granted. | Machine used. | Where qualified. |
|---|---|---|---|---|
| 1 | J. T. C. MOORE-BRABAZON | 8th Mar., 1910 | Short Biplane | Shellbeach |
| *2 | HON. C. S. ROLLS | 8th Mar., 1910 | Short Wright Biplane | Shellbeach |
| 3 | A. RAWLINSON | 5th April, 1910 | Farman Biplane | Shellbeach |
| *4 | CECIL S. GRACE | 12th April, 1910 | Short Wright Biplane | Eastchurch |
| 5 | G. B. COCKBURN | 26th April, 1910 | Farman Biplane | |
| 6 | CLAUDE GRAHAME-WHITE | 26th April, 1910 | Blériot Monoplane | Pau |
| 7 | A. OGILVIE | 24th May, 1910 | Short Wright Biplane | Camber, Rye |
| 8 | A. M. SINGER | 31st May, 1910 | Farman Biplane | |
| *9 | S. F. CODY | 7th June, 1910 | Cody Biplane | |
| 10 | LIEUT. L. D. L. GIBBS, R.F.A. | 7th June, 1910 | Farman Biplane | Mourmelon |
| 11 | HON. MAURICE EGERTON | 14th June, 1910 | Short Wright Biplane | Eastchurch |
| 12 | JAMES RADLEY | 14th June, 1910 | Blériot Monoplane | Brooklands |
| 13 | HON. ALAN BOYLE | 14th June, 1910 | Avis Monoplane | Brooklands |
| 14 | J. ARMSTRONG DREXEL | 21st June, 1910 | Blériot Monoplane | Beaulieu |
| 15 | G. C. COLMORE | 21st June, 1910 | Short Biplane | Eastchurch |
| 16 | G. A. BARNES | 21st June, 1910 | Humber Monoplane | Brooklands |
| 17 | CAPT. GEO. DAWES | 26th July, 1910 | Humber Monoplane | Wolverhampton |
| 18 | A. V. ROE | 26th July, 1910 | Roe Triplane | |
| 19 | A. E. GEORGE | 6th Sept., 1910 | George and Jobling Biplane | Eastchurch |
| 20 | R. WICKHAM | 20th Sept., 1910 | Sommer Biplane | Brooklands |

AVIATORS' CERTIFICATES GRANTED BY THE ROYAL AERO CLUB OF THE UNITED KINGDOM

* Deceased.

The results show his certificate number and the type of plane he flew, as well as the date when the certificate was granted. In this particular case there is also a 'Deceased by' field which could help to track down death records.

The original Royal Aero Club record (right) is available by clicking on the icon. Also, in some cases, as here, more information is available: TheGenealogist has linked biographies of the early aviators from contemporary accounts where possible, including books and newspapers. Sometimes there are even photographs available.

Cody's biography tells of his upbringing in Iowa, USA, where he learned the cowboy skills which led to him touring England with his Wild West act, trading on the name of Buffalo Bill Cody (no relation). He then became an early pioneer of manned flight, most famous for his work on the Cody War-Kites that were used in World War One as a smaller alternative to balloons for artillery spotting.

He was also the first man to conduct a powered flight in Britain, on 16 October 1908.

He died in a plane accident in August 1913.

website TheGenealogist and offer a fascinating insight into the pioneer years of British aviation. Sadly, they also reveal that of the first 20 people to be granted a certificate, three were dead from accidents by 1914, including the US-born aviation pioneer Samuel F Cody (see the case study above).

The Club was hugely influential in these fledgling days, and its members included and indeed trained most military pilots (more than 6,300 of them) until 1915 when military flying schools were established.

The Club was responsible for UK control of all private and sporting flying, as well as records and competitions, and continues to represent recreational flying in Britain today.

Those early certificates also list the types of plane each aviator flew. A popular early choice, including that of Moore-Brabazon, was the Short Biplane.

The Short brothers, Eustace and Oswald, started out as balloon manufacturers at the turn of the 20th century, but after hearing reports of the Wright brothers' first flight in France in 1908, they moved into plane manufacture. Oswald is reported to have declared: "This is the finish of ballooning: we must begin building aeroplanes at once!" They persuaded a third brother, Horace, to join the team.

The Short No. 1 Biplane was exhibited at the first British Aero Show, held at Olympia in London. The No. 2 edition was built for Moore-Brabazon and in November 1909 he used it to win a £1000 Daily Mail competition to complete the first closed-circuit flight of more than a mile in a British aircraft.

Although Moore-Brabazon gave up his personal aviation career, he remained closely connected with the growing importance of flight. In World War One he became a pioneer of aerial photography and an early member of the Royal Air Force. After the war he became a Conservative MP and in World War Two he served as Minister of Transport and then Minister of Aircraft Production. He was also the instigator of the airgraph communication system (see Issue 2 of the Discover Your Ancestors bookazine for a feature on that subject).

Early aviation in Britain was a classic example of the realm of gentlemen amateurs of private means. Of the first five Aero Club certificate holders, three were from titled backgrounds; one was from America; and only one, George Cockburn, was of more ordinary origins, the son of a Liverpool merchant.

Exploring these early aviators' lives via these online certificates and biographies provides a fascinating window into what was perhaps the last pioneering era of modern times.

# Back to paper

*Simon Fowler explains how to find records that aren't available online yet... and the internet can still help the process*

The fatal flaw in doing family history through the internet is the temptation to think that everything is online. But it is not true. The National Archives (TNA) estimates that only 5% of its records have been digitised. They are being slightly disingenuous, as all the major sources for genealogical research at Kew are now online, although there are still significant exceptions. These include Army officers' records, Army and Navy muster rolls, Metropolitan Police service registers and Poor Law correspondence.

The proportion of records online at local record offices is rather lower – perhaps 2-3% per cent. However, this is changing rapidly, as the big data websites index and scan parish registers and related material in the parish chest.

But there are always going to be records that the commercial data providers will never copy, because they are too difficult to digitise and index. Court records at local archives, for example – particularly quarter and petty sessions – are name rich, but are hard to use, so won't necessarily be copied.

It can be hard enough to find what you want online, so you'd think it would be much harder to discover what records are available where at Britain's hundreds of archives. But in fact it is dead easy – and it can all be done online.

Did I say hundreds of archives? I meant thousands, from internationally important places such as The National Archives and the Public Record Office of Northern Ireland to tiny repositories such as Barings Bank Archives, where you share a desk with the archivist. There are 400 alone in London.

Details of virtually all of them are available through 'Find an archive' at TNA's website (**http://discovery.nationalarchives.gov.uk/find-an-archive**). This will give you an address, a link to the archive's website, and details of opening hours. It is also up to date.

There are also separate databases for Wales, **www.archivesnetwork-wales.info**, and Scotland, **www.scan.org.uk**. See also The National Register of Archives for Scotland – **www.nas.gov.uk/nras**.

But remember that if you've searched and can't find anything about your ancestor, it doesn't mean that there isn't anything about them. It's just that their name hasn't been picked up in the indexes.

There are also several more specialist databases. If you are interested in ancestors who worked in hospitals (or who were patients) and know which hospital they were in, check out **www.nationalarchives.gov.uk/ hospitalrecords**. The Manorial Documents Register – **http://discovery.nationalarchives.gov.uk/manor-search** – has details of manorial records, which can be very useful if your forebears were farmers.

The excellent Army Museum Ogilby Trust – **www.armymuseums.org.uk** – provides links to regimental museums and archives. Lastly the Archives Hub has details of university archives – **http://archiveshub.ac.uk**. Even if you haven't got a don on the family tree, the Hub has lots of very interesting articles on the use that can be made of archives in general.

Every record office has a website. Most provide downloadable guides to their holdings, usually written with family and local historians in mind. And many now provide online catalogues, which enhance and improve upon Access to Archives mentioned above.

That's the good news. The bad is that they can be difficult to use. In part because they are generally designed by archivists for use by archivists rather than the rest of us!

The best I've come across is SEAX at the Essex Record Office, where you just type a name or phrase into the search engine and it goes away and finds the answer – **http://seax.essexcc.gov.uk/**.

More often you need to think about exactly what you are looking for and use modifiers to try to find the answer. To prevent a great deal of frustration it is always a good idea to read the instructions before starting out.

But remember – and it is a point worth repeating – just because you've done a search for a particular ancestor in the search engine and nothing comes up, it does not mean that there is nothing about him.

As an example from my own research, take Charles Gretton, who was an officer in the West Essex Militia. SEAX shows there are no documents about him – but a lot can be found about him in the many records of the militia at the Essex Record Office.

Clearly, if the records themselves are offline, then you have to visit the archives to look at them for yourself. If you can't get there you might want to use a professional researcher to do the work. There's a list of reputable researchers who are members of the Association of Genealogists and Researchers in Archives at **www.agra.org.uk**.

As well as The National Archives, each English and Welsh county has its own record office. But many Welsh records are also with the National Library of Wales in Aberystwyth (**www.llgc.org/uk**). There are fewer local record offices in Scotland so you may wish to start with the National Records of Scotland (**www.nas.gov.uk**). In Northern Ireland almost all archives are with PRONI (the Public Record Office of Northern Ireland – **www.proni.gov.uk**).

Each record office is different. As well as leaflets and catalogues their websites should provide advice to visitors: simple things like opening hours and parking.

The important thing is to allow plenty of time to find your feet – particularly if you have never been to a record office before.

Do talk to the staff about your research interests. Don't be bashful – they have heard all the stupid questions already. More seriously, they can give tips and pointers that can save you hours of wasted time.

But it is worth persevering. There is nothing like the thrill of handling a document written or signed by an ancestor. And this thrill can never be replicated by a digitised scan, however good!

**SIMON FOWLER** is a professional history researcher and writer. Find out more at www.history-man.co.uk.

---

# VISITING AN ARCHIVE

If you're making your first visit to an archive, it's worth familiarising yourself with the setup – there is usually information available at the record office's website. Some general pointers:

- take a pencil: most archives don't allow the use of pens to avoid risking damage to old books and documents
- bring some small change if you are likely to need photocopying services. Many archives will have dedicated machines for copying pages from microfilm or microfiche – the staff can help you get started with them
- many archives allow you to bring a digital camera to take pictures of documents you find, but there may be a charge – make sure you know the rules before you start snapping!
- don't forget to turn your phone off or put it in a locker
- check beforehand whether you need to book: at most larger archives and record offices you can usually just turn up, but visiting smaller archives or special collections within the larger centres may require an appointment
- allow extra time for administration when you arrive: you may not just be able to dive into the records! Many record offices will require you to fill in a form for a reader's card first – and you may need identification such as a driving licence and bank statement
- look into the CARN (County Archives Research Network) scheme – see www.archives.org.uk/general/county-archive-research-network-carn.html. Around 60 record offices in England and Wales support this: one card gets you into all of them.

# Suffer the little children?

*For centuries, child labour was a reality for our ancestors. Sharon Brookshaw explores how a childhood of play is very much a modern invention*

When we think of our ancestors, we tend to picture them as adults. If we think of children in the past at all, we often imagine the Victorian schoolroom, a stricter form of education than we are familiar with today, but education nonetheless. However, in 1840 only an estimated 20% of London's children had any formal schooling, a number that rose to around half by 1860; it was doubtfully any higher in the rest of the country. What were the rest of the children doing?

For children of poor and working class families – who would have made up the majority of the population – working had for centuries been the norm. The idea of children working was not particularly controver-

**An illustration of child brick workers, by Herbert Johnson of *The Graphic*. The children often had to queue in pubs to be paid. A report in *The Graphic* observed: "Sometimes the children have to wait for hours before they receive their money, and not infrequently they are made completely drunk while so waiting."**

# CHILD WORKERS IN THE CENSUSES

Data from the decennial censuses offers a fascinating snapshot of child labour through the 19th century. All of the censuses from 1841 to 1911 are available online, fully indexed, at **www.thegenealogist.co.uk**.

This full indexing means it's possible to analyse the records very precisely.

For example, an analysis by the team at TheGenealogist reveals the top occupations for children aged 13 years or younger in the Durham 1841 census included the following (in descending order): female servant, coal miner, agricultural labourer, male servant, apprentice, pitman, labourer, collier, lead miner, tailor apprentice, worsted spinner, shoe maker apprentice, spinner, factory worker, blacksmith, farmer.

Compare this with a similar list for Essex in the same year: agricultural labourer, female servant, labourer, male servant, silk weaver, farmer, servant, tambourer (an embroiderer), carpenter, gardener, weaver, silk winder, silk throwster, apprentice, shoe maker, fisherman, brick layer.

These lists show the important industries in the regions – mining in Durham, farming in Essex (around 2000 agricultural labourers compared to little over 100 in Durham) – and more generally that the Essex occupations seem on the whole to be considerably gentler than those typical in Durham. Interestingly for two counties with a similar total population (between 320,000 and 340,000), the census suggests there were three times as many child workers in Essex as in Durham. However, the number of children listed as a 'pupil' in Essex is 940, compared to only 157 in Durham.

sial in pre-industrial Britain. Indeed, John Wesley, the founder of Methodism, thought that it prevented youthful idleness and vice. Children would help with simple household tasks as soon as they were old enough to be physically capable of doing so. As they got older, they could take on jobs more important to the household economy, such as planting and harvesting crops, assisting with the family's cottage industry, or otherwise working outside the home as domestic servants or by taking an apprenticeship.

As apprentices, children lived and worked with a master to learn his trade, receiving training, board and lodging in place of wages. While the age of being bound to a master could be as young as seven in some parishes and industries, it could also be anything up to the late teens in other cases, depending on circumstances. Children typically stayed for seven years until at least the age of 21 when they would be expert enough to be considered a 'journeyman' and work independently. This was considered to be a fair deal by parents, children and masters alike, and the details of these pacts were set down in documents called indentures. From 1601, the Poor Relief Act allowed parish officials to bind the poorest children to masters. By paying for these children to be apprenticed, parishes hoped to save the cost of their maintenance in later life.

By the late 18th century, the growing pace of the Industrial Revolution caused drastic changes to the nature of employment in Britain. The appearance of the first textile mills saw children recruited as primary workers, despite still being called apprentices. A conservative estimate is that in 1784 one third of the total workers in rural mills were apprentices and their numbers reached as high as 80-90% in some individual mills. The reasons for this were a mixture of adult labour shortages, poverty, and a ready supply of children in parish workhouses and orphanages who could be cheaply indentured. By conditioning children to factory life at an early age, mill owners could also potentially retain a reliable, disciplined workforce for years to come.

What was it like for the children who worked in what William Blake called the "dark Satanic mills"? Mill worker Robert Blincoe described the lot of the child apprentice to the Factory Commission in 1833 thus: "there is the heat and dust; there are so many different forms of cruelty used upon them; then they are so liable to have their fingers catched and to suffer other accidents from the machinery...I would not have a child of mine there."

At Quarry Bank Mill in Cheshire, the Greg family ran an apprentice house close to their mill between 1790 and 1847, which could house up to 100 children at any one time – the majority of whom were girls, as the Gregs thought them "less truculent" than boys. Children could be taken on as young as nine, and their apprenticeship lasted until 18. They all worked 12-hour shifts in the mill, starting at 6am and finishing at 7pm, with an hour's break for dinner at noon. After factory work had ended for the day, the apprentices had domestic chores to complete before finally being locked in their dormitories for the night.

The employment rates of children in textile factories continued to be high until the mid-19th century. A parliamentary report published in 1834 shows that as much as 20% of the mill workforce in textile towns consisted of children under the age of 14. In both the 1841 and 1851 censuses, 'cotton manufacture' was still among the top three occupations for both boys and girls under 15. But the phrase 'in textile towns' is significant – the employment of children in textile mills, while high, was a regional phenomenon.

In other areas, children made up significant proportions of the workforce in coal and metal mines. In Cornish tin mines, for example, there were an estimated 7,000 children employed in 1839. Mining was commonly a family affair; until the age of 12, children usually worked on the surface, perhaps sweeping or dressing ore, but later the boys could follow their fathers into the mines. The work was dirty, dangerous and uncertain, but usually better paid than working in agriculture or fishing. Others were employed as "climbing boys" for chimney sweeps, the subject of the first labour law to mention children in 1788. This specified a minimum age of eight for these boys, but was not well enforced.

During the second half of the 19th century, the number of child workers gradually declined, although by 1881, children under 15 still made up 11% of the British workforce. This decline was partly due to the succession of Factory Acts passed during the 19th century to reduce the hours and improve the conditions of child workers, making them more expensive to employ, and the development of heavier or more complicated technology in some industries that required adult labour to operate. The system of parish indentures for pauper children was also brought to an end in 1844, cutting off a ready supply of child workers.

The growth of educational reform also took off at this time. In the late 18th and early 19th centuries, there existed only a handful of schools for working class children, and attendance was difficult for those who worked daily. The establishment of the Ragged School Union in 1844 – so called because the pupils were too raggedly dressed to be able to attend any other school – saw the first organised attempt to provide regular education for poor children. However, it was not until 1870 that

# CHILDREN IN THE BRICKWORKS

A pair of articles in The Graphic newspaper of 1871 revealed the ongoing horrors of child labour in the brickworks of England. The Factory Acts of the early and mid-19th century had regulated children's hours and conditions of employment in the textile industry, but only in other industries from 1878. The author wrote: "... at the present moment there are in our various brick-fields and brick-works, between 20,000 and 30,000 children, from the ages of three and four up to sixteen, undergoing what has been expressively described as 'a very bondage of toil and a horror of evil-training that carries peril in it'."

A leading campaigner against these horrors was George Smith, who wrote various pamphlets on the subject. Smith had experienced this work as a child himself, and described it vividly: "The children were of various ages, from nine to twelve, but mostly nine to ten. They were of both sexes, and in a half-naked state. Their employment consisted in carrying the damp clay on their heads to the brick-makers, and carrying the made bricks to the 'floors' on which they are placed to dry. Their employment lasts thirteen hours daily, during which they traverse a distance of about twenty miles... Imagine a child of nine or ten, with features prematurely old, toiling from six in the morning until seven in the evening, and receiving nothing but curses and blows from the men, because he is not quick enough in his movements. What is it but actual slavery of the worst description?"

Smith also demonstrated how each child typically had to carry 43 pounds of clay on his head for more that six miles at a stretch. He wrote: "The total quantity of clay thus carried by me was five and a half tons. For all this labour I received sixpence!"

compulsory education for children was made law in England and Wales, and the act only required the provision of education up to age 10.

Even as children became schoolchildren rather than apprentices and employees, they continued to make significant contributions by working. During World War One, some sold small items as part of schemes to raise money for refugees, while others filled in the vacancies left by the 60,000 agricultural workers who had gone to war. The services of the Boy Scouts were offered by Robert Baden-Powell; they watched coastlines, reservoirs and telegraphs to prevent sabotage, acted as messengers and aided the coastguards. Some even went to France to serve refreshments to troops. By December 1914, it was estimated that 100,000 Scouts had been employed in war work. The Girl Guides also played their part by training as volunteer nurses.

Children became unpaid agricultural workers in World War Two as well. From 1940, harvest camps were established by the Ministry of Agriculture for both adults and children. By 1949, 249 camps had successfully housed over 8,000 urban boys who had helped filled the harvest-time employment gap in the countryside. Separate camps were established for girls, with over 20,000 attending in 1943 alone. Additionally, rural children would also have joined in farm work. Farmers were full of praise for the child workers, and while utilising this source of labour may have seemed like exploitation to some, it is doubtful how much of the wartime harvest would have been planted, let alone harvested, without the work of children.

As the length of compulsory schooling continued to increase – to 14 in 1918, 15 in 1944 and 16 in 1972 – the nature of children's work shrank and is now largely confined to school homework and Saturday jobs. However, the huge amount of work that has been undertaken in the past by children should not be forgotten. If our ancestors weren't working as children, they may well have been employing them.

**SHARON BROOKSHAW** studied archaeology at Durham and has postgraduate degrees from the International Centre for Cultural and Heritage Studies, University of Newcastle upon Tyne.

# Joining the dots

*Powerful tools online can help you link birth, marriage and death records – and the censuses – together*

Family history is of course about making connections between people, parent to child, spouse to spouse, as we gradually piece together a family tree.

What can often help shed new light on those connections, get past problems and open up new avenues of research is making connections between different types of record, too.

In this article we'll look specifically at birth, marriage and death records since civil registration began in 1837 (for England and Wales). This time span means that in theory you can piece together as many as six generations of one family.

You can search all the BMD indexes from 2005 right back to 1837 at **www.thegenealogist.co.uk**. Traditionally the indexes have only been seen as useful for ordering the full certificates, but TheGenealogist's SmartSearch technology has now opened them up as a much more useful resource in themselves.

The actual certificates, of course, can then yield even more information

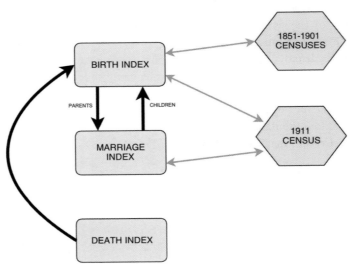

**Making connections with SmartSearch: TheGenealogist's unique technology finds the links between BMD records, and with the censuses, without even needing to order full certificates**

for your research. (These are not online as a government plan to digitise them ground to a halt a few years ago: you will need to order them from the General Register Office for a fee, currently £9.25 for the standard service – see **www.gro.gov.uk.**)

The basic indexes for births, marriages and deaths from 1 July 1837 onwards all have a similar fomat. They provide a person's first name and surname, and initials for any middle names (earlier indexes sometimes had these in full).

Also detailed are the registration district where the event was registered and a reference number, plus the quarter of the year when the birth was registered (or the month from 1983).

The numbers of regions, districts and subdistricts have changed over time – in some cases these details can help confirm whether you have the right ancestor. You can find a full list of districts and their changes at **www.ukbmd.org.uk/genuki/reg**. Also useful to know is that from 1841 the district was the same as that for census enumeration, making it easier to cross-refer between BMDs and census records.

Even the reference code can be useful in occasional cases: in birth indexes it would establish the likelihood of twins, for example.

All three types of index saw changes in later decades which provided extra information and prove powerful in connecting records together.

In birth indexes, from September 1911 onwards the mother's maiden name was included, which of course is an immediate way to connect back to the mother as well as the father.

The district might also provide a clue to tracing the parents' marriage record. The easiest way to do this is using the SmartSearch system at TheGenealogist (see the case study on page 19) – potential parents can be listed at a click of a button, with far more precise results from 1911 onwards due to the mother's maiden name field. If you think your ancestors didn't move much, you may find the parents' marriage in the same district as the birth – but of course you may not, in which case the SmartSearch results will still give you strong leads to follow.

As for the actual birth certificates, these of course provide more detail. This includes the name and surname of both father and mother (maiden name), which will provide the strongest links for following them up in marriage records and of course back to their own births. This is assuming both names were given at the time – illegitimate births may have a blank where the father's name should be, for example (thus the surname in a pre-1911 index could in some cases be that of the mother rather than the father).

Other essential information you will gain from the birth certificate itself includes the precise date of birth (bear in mind that registration could have taken place a few weeks later, and even be listed in the following quarter), full name and the father's occupation. The column for details of the informant can confirm where the family was living, or list another member of the family to follow up in BMD and other records.

If there's a gap between the dates of birth and registration, it could indicate illness or that the child was not born where the family usually resided.

All of this information, including father's occupation, could help corroborate findings in contemporary census records (all of those available for England and Wales, from 1841 to 1911, are also at **www.thegenealogist.co.uk**). It works the other way round, too: TheGenealogist has built SmartSearch into all of the censuses from 1851 to 1911 inclusive, so you can find potential children of a marriage. For the 1911 census only, you can even link straight to potential marriage indexes for a husband and wife in the household.

Moving on to marriages, the indexes effectively list the marriage twice: once under the groom's name, and once under the bride's maiden name. From the second quarter of 1912 onwards, in each case a second column lists just the surname of the other party – so you can check both to be cast iron sure there hasn't been an error somewhere (rare, but not impossible). This also means you can find out the other spouse's first name.

Once again, SmartSearch at TheGenealogist can straight away connect you to other family members: every marriage index entry will take you to a list of potential children of the marriage (more accurate from September 1911 again because of both parents' surnames being listed in the birth index).

The marriage certificate itself (technically, what you order from the GRO is a copy) then provides strong leads for links to other records. Most notably it will give you the ages of both parties – assuming they told the truth! You can then follow these up in birth indexes if they don't take you beyond 1837; otherwise your first port of call would be parish records. Aiding this will be the marriage certificate's column for the names of the fathers of each spouse – and of course they take you back a generation anyway. Earlier marriages may just say 'of full age' (ie 21 or over), mind, which will make your connecting work rather harder!

# SMARTSEARCH IN ACTION

TheGenealogist is the only website with SmartSearch technology linking all BMD indexes together. These enable you to find potential parents from a birth, potential children to a marriage and potential birth records from a death record. All three types of index have now been fully digitised from 2005 back to 1837 – in fact, the death indexes have only just been completed as this issue goes to press.

Let's use the sad early death of T-Rex guitarist and vocalist Marc Bolan as a

starting point: he died when he was only 29, and his real name was Mark Feld, which we can use to search the death records. SmartSearch allows us to jump straight to his birth record, which then links to his parents and potential siblings. We can find full details of his parents Simeon and Phyllis, including their marriage record.

We can also look up Phyllis' own death record - this then gives her date of birth as 23 August 1927. We can look up her birth index from this - SmartSearch can then list potential siblings. Her mother's maiden name was Pither: now we can also look up her own parents' marriage using SmartSearch. Leonard Atkins and Elsie Pither married in 1920 - so we can then push back their lives into the era of the censuses, and so on.

Traditionally tracing female relatives has been very hard, but where marriages took place after 1911 SmartSearch makes it impressively easy.

Finally, other useful information in the certificate includes whether each party had been married before (which could help find a previous marriage record or even one for a divorce), their occupation and that of their father.

With death indexes, once again there were changes which provide useful extra info. In this case, the age of the deceased was provided from March 1866, and this was replaced by their precise date of birth from March 1969. Either way, the obvious link is then to birth records – and once again TheGenealogist's SmartSearch makes the most of this, by automating the birth search for you. (Naturally, for deaths before 1869 the chances of finding the birth index by this means are less likely, given the lack of age information, and in any case they would have had to have died young.)

The full death certificate then adds when and where the person died (a potential link to censuses), age, occupation and cause of death. A field for the name and address of the informant can be helpful – it may just be the deceased's doctor, but of course it could also be a spouse or a family member to follow up in other records.

One final comment: civil registration was only compulsory after 1875, and with births in particular as many as a third were probably not registered between 1837 and then, so you can't always guarantee finding your ancestor.

But if you do, you can now see there are myriad ways of connecting them to other BMD records (even if you don't want to pay for the full certificates) and indeed other records, especially censuses and parish registers.

# Voting for action

*Only a century ago, women were starving themselves and worse just to get the vote. Nell Darby tells the story of the suffragettes*

A century ago, on 5 June 1913, Emily Wilding Davison died while trying to throw a banner over King George V's horse at the Epsom Derby. Emily's action – either heroic or reckless, depending on your viewpoint – is one of the most iconic images of the suffragettes' long struggle to win women the vote.

But Emily's attempt to get the public's attention over the issue of women's right to vote was just one small part of a long and eventually successful campaign that took place over the late 19th and early 20th centuries. Many women involved in the fight were prepared to do anything to advance their cause – including starving themselves, being arrested and imprisoned, and lampooned in the press.

The suffragettes were a collection of women, largely from upper and middle-class backgrounds, and including many teachers, who were frustrated by the limitations that society and government put on them due to their gender. Although some men, such as John Stuart Mill, had first proposed women's suffrage back in 1865, it would be decades before

**Christabel Pankhurst inviting the public to 'rush' the House of Commons at a meeting in Trafalgar Square in October 1908**

# THE DISILLUSIONED SUFFRAGETTE

Dora Marsden was a Yorkshire-born suffragette who, although not quite as well known as the Pankhursts or Emily Davison, was involved in both peaceful and militant action with the Women's Social and Political Union.

The 1881 census (available at **www.thegenealogist.co.uk**) shows her parents, Fred and Hannah, living at The Step in Marsden, Yorkshire, where Dora was born the following year. Her father deserted the family in 1890 and emigrated

**The arrest of Dora Marsden outside Manchester University on 4 October 1909**

to America, leaving her mother Hannah to support her children by working as a seamstress.

According to the Dictionary of National Biography (**www.oxforddnb.com**) Dora won a scholarship to enter Owens College, Manchester – later Manchester University – in 1900 and graduated with a 2:i in 1903, by this point having become part of a group of feminists in Manchester who included Christabel Pankhurst.

The Times Digital Archive (available in some libraries) shows that on 31 March 1909, Dora, together with other suffragettes, took part in an attempt to force an entrance to the House of Commons, and was arrested. On 1 April, The Times recorded that Dora had been charged with assaulting the police. Six months later, The Times reported that Dora had created a disturbance outside Manchester University while Lord Morley was delivering an address, and she was again arrested.

However, Dora became disillusioned with the WSPU's leadership – which was firmly focused on the Pankhursts – and withdrew from political activity in 1913. She had a nervous breakdown in 1934 and, suffering from a psychotic depression, was admitted to hospital in Dumfries, where she died in 1960.

women – and some men – joined forces in an organised movement to argue for women's right to vote.

In 1897, Millicent Fawcett set up the Union of Women's Suffrage Societies – a collection of local groups – to campaign for voting rights through the writing and distribution of leaflets and petitions. The Union had a limited effect, however, and in 1903 Emmeline Pankhurst established the Women's Social and Political Union (WSPU).

Emmeline believed that any movement needed to be both radical and militant if it was going to have any effect; but the willingness of members to use violence if necessary was seen as proof in some quarters that women were too illogical and hysterical to deserve the vote. Journalist Charles E Hands, writing in the Daily Mail, coined the term 'suffragette' to describe this new breed of militant protestor.

From 1905, the suffragettes attempted to gain publicity through peaceful protests. These sometimes led to arrests on what seem, to modern eyes, to be absurdly trivial charges. For example, in 1909 a 61-year-old nurse, Elise Evans, was charged with "wilfully and persistently causing an obstruction". Her crime had been to chalk the phrase 'Votes for Women' on the pavement on the Strand. She was fined 20 shillings.

In 1908, the WSPU decided to try and enter the House of Commons in order to approach the Prime Minister, Herbert Asquith, and argue their cause. Emmeline and Christabel Pankhurst spoke at a public meeting in Trafalgar Square beforehand, stressing that they wanted to remain non-violent. They asked women to come "unarmed and without sticks or stones" to give their support, producing a handbill to this effect. The Pankhursts were then issued with a summons, accusing them of "conduct likely to provoke a breach of the peace" – it being argued that the handbill had incited the public "to do a certain wrongful and illegal act" in storming the Commons.

By the time they tried again to storm the Commons, in 1911, the suffragettes' tactics had changed. On 21 November, a group from the WSPU again tried to storm the building – this time armed with stones and hammers. Their action illustrated a militant phase of the campaign

# IN AND OUT OF THE 1911 CENSUS

The UK 1911 census, which took place on Sunday 2 April, coincided with the peak period of activism for the suffragettes. Many of them used it as an opportunity to protest.

It is estimated that several thousand women may have chosen to boycott the 1911 census, in some cases avoiding the enumerators by packing in large numbers into hidden rooms or lurking in sheds and barns.

However, many also used the census forms as an opportunity to express themselves, as excellent quality images from the 1911 census collection at data website The Genealogist (**www.thegenealogist.co.uk**) reveal. The pictures shown here reveal how many women defaced the census forms. Others (who can be found using the site's keyword search) wrote heartfelt statements of their frustration. For example, an Isabella Leo in London wrote: "If I am intelligent enough to fill in this census form, I can surely make a X on a ballot paper."

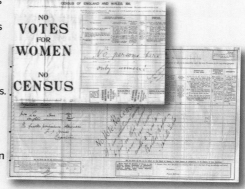

to get votes for women. This behaviour also saw some suffragettes chaining themselves to railings, committing acts of arson, and smashing windows, as well as organising marches on Parliament. It has been estimated that in the period up to 1914, around a thousand suffragettes were imprisoned in England.

The suffragettes, under the WSPU banner, lobbied to get their arrested and convicted members recognised as political prisoners. This would give them better treatment in prison, including being allowed frequent visits. However, they were unsuccessful, and failed to be given any

# RESEARCHING THE SUFFRAGETTES

If you are trying to locate a suffragette ancestor, your first port of call should be The National Archives (TNA). It has several records relating to the suffragist movement, located mainly within its Metropolitan Police and Home Office collections. For example, in the former collection, there is a list of suffragette complaints against the police in 1911 (MEPO 3/203), and a history of the suffragette movement (MEPO 2/1145).

In the Home Office papers, there are details of the suffragettes' treatment in prison, and the remission of some of their prison sentences, dating from 1922 (HO 45/11088/437465). There is also a report on the picketing of Downing Street by women who were subsequently convicted of obstruction (HO 144/1038/181250), and the raiding of a suffragette's flat in Maida Vale, West London, which was being used as the headquarters of the Women's Social and Political Union in 1913 (HO 45/10695/231366).

Not all of the records relate to the capital; there are details of the imprisonment of nine suffragettes in Birmingham's Winson Green Prison in September 1909, following their protests when Prime Minister Herbert Asquith visited the city (HO 45/10417/183577). One of the women involved in this protest was Laura Ainsworth, who was then sent to Winson Green for 14 days, during which time she had gone on hunger strike. The authorities deliberately released her early in the morning of 5 October – just before 7am instead of the usual 8.30am – in order to avoid her receiving publicity or support from other suffragettes. Although The Times noted that despite having undergone forced feeding, "she appeared very little the worse for her experience" – a statement somewhat undermined by the subsequent comment that she was taken straight from prison to a nursing home to recuperate. Her first forced feeding involved being placed in a chair "and her head forcibly held back, her mouth was forced open, four or five wardresses held her in the chair and milk was poured down her through a feeding cup". The next day, she refused to take the cup and so a tube was "pushed into the mouth and down the throat; a cork gag was placed between the teeth so as to keep the mouth open, and four wardresses held her". This was carried out twice a day, with meat extract forced through her teeth at lunchtimes.

This article shows how newspapers – both national and local – can be an invaluable source of information about individual suffragettes and their actions. The Times Digital Archive, accessible through local libraries, is a useful first site, as is the British Newspaper Archive.

In terms of books, The Ascent of Woman: A History of the Suffragette Movement by Melanie Phillips (Abacus, 2004), The British Suffrage Campaign: 1866-1928 by Harold Smith (Longman, 2009), and Women in England 1760-1914 by Susie Steinbach (Phoenix, 2005) are all worth a read. If you are looking to research a suffragette ancestor's life, try reading Jennifer Newby's Women's Lives: Researching Women's Social History 1800-1939 (Pen & Sword, 2011).

privileges due to their social or political position. This led to some suffragettes starting hunger strikes in prison – the first woman to do so being Marion Wallace Dunlop, who had been imprisoned in Holloway back in 1909 after being convicted of vandalism. Dunlop's hunger strike continued for 91 hours; the Government feared that she might become a martyr and the Home Office duly released her from prison early on medical grounds. Others then started hunger strikes in order to also get released early.

The WSPU saw its hunger strikers as heroines; a banner produced in 1910 contains the signatures of 80 such women, who had "faced death without flinching". The government attempted to deal with the phenomenon of hunger striking women, as well as those women who purposely starved themselves in order to get released from prison. In 1913, the Prisoners (Temporary Discharge for Ill-health) Act – commonly known as the Cat and Mouse Act – was passed, enabling prisoners on hunger strike to be temporarily released from prison until they had regained their health. At that point, they could be rearrested and made to continue their prison sentence.

The lead-up to the World War One had a major impact on the acts of the suffragettes. Many focused their attention on the war effort, hunger strikes largely stopped, and in the summer of 1914, all suffrage prisoners were released on an amnesty, with Emmeline Pankhurst ending militant activities soon after. Politicians had felt that the suffragettes' militant activities actually antagonised public opinion; so when they started focusing on the war effort, and publicising their activities in this field, public opinion started to turn. Partial enfranchisement of women occurred at the end of the war, in 1918. In February that year, the Representation of the People Act let women over 30 who also met minimum property qualifications get the vote. Seven months later, women were allowed to become MPs. However, it took another decade before the 1928 Representation of the People Act made women equal to men, letting anyone over 21 eligible to vote. The suffragist movement had been long and sometimes violent; but ultimately the suffragettes were successful in their aims.

**NELL DARBY** is a freelance writer, specialising in social history and the history of crime. She has a PhD in gender and the summary process in the 18th century.

# Operation Chastise

*Records of the famous Dam Busters raids are available online*

On the night of 16/17 May, 1943, 19 aircraft of Royal Air Force No 617 Squadron took off to breach a number of important dams in and around the Ruhr area of Germany. There were three primary targets, namely the Möhne, Eder and Sorpe dams, and three alternative targets, the Lister, Ennerpe and Diemel dams.

Of those 19 aircraft, eight failed to return. The attack was considered an outstanding success in spite of these losses, and the Eder and the Möhne dams were breached, and the Sorpe damaged. This was Operation Chastise, which made No 617 Squadron famous ever afterwards as the 'Dam Busters'.

Now the ever-expanding data website TheGenealogist (**www.thegenealogist.co.uk**) has digitised records of this daring raid and made them available online to subscribers.

Prior to the start of the war, the British Air Ministry had identified Germany's heavily industrialised Ruhr Valley and especially the dams as important strategic targets. Repeated air strikes with large bombs could be effective but Bomber Command had struggled for accuracy in the face of heavy enemy fire.

Finally Operation Chastise was devised using a specially designed 'bouncing bomb' invented and developed by British engineer Barnes Wallis.

The operation was tasked to No 5 Group RAF, which formed a new squadron to undertake the mission. Led by 24-year-old Wing Commander Guy Gibson, a veteran of more than 170 bombing and night-fighter missions, 21 bomber crews were selected from existing squadrons in 5 Group. These crews included RAF personnel of several different nationalities, as well as members of the Royal Australian Air Force (RAAF), Royal Canadian Air Force (RCAF) and Royal New Zealand Air Force (RNZAF). The squadron was based at RAF Scampton, about five miles north of Lincoln.

The attack was divided into three waves. The first wave of nine aircraft subdivided into three sections of three aircraft each, took off at 10 minute intervals, in perfectly clear weather, and with a full moon to assist them. They were detailed for the Möhne and the Eder dams, in that order of priority. The second wave, consisting of five aircraft, took off to attack the Sorpe Dam, taking a different route, but timed to cross the enemy coast at the same time. The third wave, consisting of the remaining five aircraft, formed an air bomb reserve and took off three hours later, each detailed for one of the alternative targets.

Of the five aircraft detailed to attack the Sorpe dam, two returned early, one is known to have attacked, and two went missing without trace. A sixth aircraft from the mobile reserve was also detailed to attack the target, and did so successfully.

**The crew of Lancaster ED285/'AJ-T' pictured at RAF Scampton, Lincolnshire on 22 July 1943. From left: Sergeant G Johnson; Pilot Officer D A MacLean, navigator; Flight Lieutenant J C McCarthy, pilot; Sergeant L Eaton, gunner. In the rear are Sergeant R Batson, gunner and Sergeant W G Ratcliffe, engineer**

Two of the remaining four aircraft of the mobile reserve were detailed to attack the Sorpe dam: one attacked successfully and one went missing, and it is believed did not attack. The fourth aircraft was detailed to attack the Lister dam, and acknowledged the order. There is no further trace of it, and it is not known if an attack took place. The fifth aircraft successfully attacked the dam at Enneppe.

The Operation Record Book now put online by TheGenealogist provides an in-depth analysis of the mission. The fascinating information includes an account of each aircraft's flight, including full crew list and details of the awards made to each of the crew members after the mission. The site's Dam Busters records also provide a brief guide to researching the crew further through records at The National Archives and other sources.

Operation Chastise was success at a very high price: 53 air crew members were killed and three taken prisoner. With the new records added at TheGenealogist, it is now possible to look at every airman involved in the raid. Commencing the story with their last training flight, to the operation itself, to the visit by the King and Queen to congratulate the surviving aircrews, all the details on the famous raids are thus now online. This will be ideal if you had a relative involved with 617 Squadron, or for anyone interested in one of the most iconic RAF missions of World War Two.

# Church or chapel?

*Worship has profoundly influenced Wales for centuries.
Beryl Evans explores how to track down ancestors in both Nonconformist and Anglican communities*

If you have Welsh roots, a key issue which will have had a major influence on their lives and the records they left behind is whether they were 'church' or 'chapel' – a distinction which remains in many Welsh communities to this day.

The Church of England was the established Church in Wales until its disestablishment in 1920 to create the Church in Wales. Many Welsh people, however, embraced Nonconformism in its many forms, reflected in the common sight of numerous chapels in most Welsh communities.

It is very likely that most people searching for ancestors in Wales will at some point come across some chapel goers in their family – the Religious Census of 1851 showed that the majority of worshippers in Wales attended Nonconformist establishments rather than Anglican churches.

In either case, the records they left should not be forgotten when searching for information before the censuses and civil registration began – and indeed afterwards, as religious records are often much more accessible than information from certificates.

Thomas Cromwell first ordered parish registers to be kept as far back as 1538; these are the records of all baptisms, marriages and burials within a parish of the established Church. Only one Welsh parish, that of

**A detail from The Welsh Funeral by David Cox, depicting a scene at Bettws-y-Coed**

---

# NONCONFORMISTS ONLINE

The Nonconformist registers (also known as non-parochial registers, as they did not necessarily tally with Anglican parishes) deposited with the Registrar General in 1837 and 1857 are now held at The National Archives (TNA), Kew in series RG4. Fortunately these are readily accessible to anyone online at the easy to use pay-per-view site **www.bmdregisters.co.uk** – the site is from the same family as The Genealogist and subscribers to Gold and Diamond packages there can also access them at **www.thegenealogist.co.uk**.

RG4 covers non-parochial registers dating from 1567 to 1858, where many Welsh chapel records can be found. Other records at the site include series RG5, with the Protestant Dissenters' Registry (which mainly focused on Baptists, Independents and Presbyterians around London but can include Welsh records) plus the nationwide Wesleyan Methodist Registry; and RG6 which has records of Quakers, including those in Wales.

All of these records can be searched at the BMD Registers site, which cleverly indexes all fields – which means you may find family members such as grandparents listed in additional information such as witnesses to a marriage. To narrow down on people from a particular area, as long as you enter a surname the Advanced Search option can be refined by place name.

---

Gwaunysgor, Flintshire has entries dating that far back. In contrast, the earliest Nonconformist register is that of the Baptists of Ilston in Gower, dating from 1649. The registers of the Church were kept in an orderly fashion, with copies being sent to the Bishop at the end of each year (bishops' transcripts). As in England, from 1754 for marriages and 1813 for baptisms and burials, printed forms in bound volumes have been used. Unfortunately, the Nonconformists were not so organised: there was no guidance from a central body or authority on how and what information to record. As a result tracing Nonconformist records offline can be difficult as they are stored in various locations including the National Library of Wales (NLW, **www.llgc.org.uk**), Aberystwyth; The National Archives (TNA, **www.nationalarchives.gov.uk**), Kew; in county archive offices; and some are still in possession of ministers or in private hands.

Nonconformism began to gather pace in Wales during the 17th century after the English Civil War, despite the Restoration of the Monarchy Act of 1660 attempting to enforce conformity to the state Church. For many years the newly labelled 'Nonconformists' met in secret places – sometimes in the open air, in farm buildings or private houses. A few chapels were built during this time of persecution, but there are very few records from this early period of Nonconformism in Wales.

Following the Toleration Act of 1689, Nonconformist meeting houses and ministers were allowed after registration at Quarter Sessions or bishops' courts. But their registers were not considered to be legal like those of the established Church; therefore, the Registrar General in 1840 invited Nonconformist chapels to submit their pre-1837 registers for authentication. These registers are now held at TNA; microfilm copies are available to view at NLW (free of charge) or via **www.bmdregisters.org.uk** – see the box below for more about the site.

After toleration, the different denominations gradually grew within Wales during the early 18th century, with the keeping of records becoming more usual from the middle of the century. These causes increased their popularity under influential ministers and religious revivals were numerous during the 18th century. Industrialisation helped the growth of Nonconformism, especially in the more populous areas of Wales. Many of the already established parish churches were located too far from the populated areas, especially in the industrial areas of south Wales – so the Nonconformists built chapels where the people actually lived.

The Church in Wales deposited its original registers at NLW in the 1950s – these have since been distributed to the appropriate county archive office. All surviving bishops' transcripts are housed at NLW, along with other records of the Church in Wales. There are microfilm copies for over 500 parishes held at NLW along with facsimile copies and transcripts of many more.

When trying to establish which registers are held where and their surviving dates, you are well advised to consult a copy of Cofrestri Plwyf Cymru/Parish Registers of Wales eds. C J Williams and J Watts-Williams (NLW, Aberystwyth 2000). It lists all parishes in Wales according to county with surviving dates for each register as well as dates for bishops' transcripts, other available copies and their location, be it at NLW, TNA, county archive offices or the Society of Genealogists library in London.

A similar volume has been published for Nonconformist registers – Cofrestri Anghydffurfiol Cymru/Nonconformist Registers of Wales ed. Dafydd Ifans (NLW, Aberystwyth, 1994). It is out of print at the moment, but shows the name of the chapel, denomination, parish, OS map reference, surviving dates of registers and their location. All deposits of Nonconformist registers have been completed voluntarily. NLW is the central archive for the Presbyterian Church in Wales, previously known as Welsh Calvinistic Methodists. The Welsh Methodist (or Wesleyan) Archive is also on deposit at the Library. Many Nonconformist records are also housed in county archive offices and their individual catalogues should be checked for availability, along with that of Archives Wales (**www.archiveswales.org.uk**).

One thing to keep in mind when tracing your Nonconformist ancestors is that following Hardwicke's Marriage Act of 1753, all marriages between

1754 and 1837 (except for those of Quakers and Jews) had to take place within the established Church – even if the couple were of Nonconformist denomination. After the Civil Registration Act from 1 July 1837, marriages were allowed to take place in a Nonconformist chapel as long as a civil registrar was present and therefore there will be separate marriage registers after this date.

Not all chapels have burial grounds: very often there is only one graveyard within a whole parish, therefore Nonconformists as well as churchgoers would be buried there and recorded in the parish burial register. I have also found that very often when a Nonconformist chapel does have its own burial ground, no register is kept. In this instance any memorial inscriptions transcribed by family history societies can become invaluable for those not able to visit in person. From early in the 20th century baptisms, marriages and burials are very often recorded in the printed annual reports of chapels.

There are numerous publications that should be consulted for a wider knowledge of Nonconformism and the established Church in Wales. Many denominations have written their own histories as well as individual churches and chapels. Search the catalogues at individual county archive offices as well as the National Library of Wales.

**BERYL EVANS** has worked at the National Library of Wales since 1985, specialising in family and local history and is currently the Research Services Manager. She is also the Archives Liaison Officer and member of the Executive of the Federation of Family History Societies.

# THE TRAVELLING PREACHER

2013 saw the 300th anniversary of the birth of Daniel Rowland, Llangeitho, one of the founders of Welsh Methodism. Born in 1713, the son of Daniel Rowland, vicar of Llangeitho and Nancwnlle and Janet his wife, he was educated apparently at Hereford grammar school, before being ordained a deacon in 1734 and as a priest in 1735 within the established Church.

Around that time he went to listen to Griffith Jones (renowned for his circulating schools) preaching at nearby Llanddewi Brefi. Soon after he began travelling throughout Wales to preach. In 1737 he met Howel Harris, another well-known Methodist leader. They joined forces and led the way for a great Methodist revival in Wales. He was a renowned preacher and made Llangeitho a Mecca for Welsh Methodists - thousands flocked there from every part of Wales on Communion Sunday. In 1863, the Bishop of St David's relieved him of his curacy at Llangeitho, and he was no longer permitted to preach in the Church. The entire congregation left with him and subsequently built a new chapel, now known as Gwynfil Chapel (Calvinistic Methodist) in the village of Llangeitho, not far from the parish church which expelled him. He continued his ministry there until his death in 1790. He was buried in the parish church, ironically, the church was extended after his death and his body now lies by the altar, where there is a memorial tablet to him in the floor. A public subscription in 1883 raised funds to erect a statue of Daniel Rowland which can be seen today next to Gwynfil Chapel, looking towards the parish church.

# The plot thickens

*A pictorial guide to how surname and other distribution maps can provide useful clues on where your ancestors came from and where they may have gone next*

Every genealogist will have come up against the proverbial 'brick wall' where a family line just vanishes into the past. Today, however, technology can sometimes provide invaluable clues thanks to crunching large amounts of data at the click of a mouse button.

The widest range of UK surname distribution maps available is at **www.thegenealogist.co.uk**, where you can plot surname maps based on either census or civil registration data.

Each has its advantages. Censuses plots will count pretty much everyone with a particular surname (including phonetic variants) alive at the time of the census – this works for all of those available for England and Wales, ie from 1841 to 1911.

Plotting BMDs for a single year will show far fewer numbers as of course it will only include events that happened in the actual year in question – but you can widen to show a year range (up to 15 years either

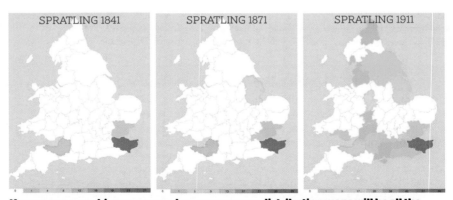

**If you are researching an unusual name, surname distribution maps will be all the more useful. Let's look at the surname 'Spratling', for example. Across the huge range of records at www.thegenealogist.co.uk, there are only a few thousand relating to this name - compared with common names which can run into the millions. The three maps above are from the site's collections of census data, from left to right 1841, 1871 and 1911 respectively. The 1841 map clearly shows how the name is strongest in Kent, with a smaller spread into Essex - but there is also what looks like a separate branch in Somerset. The 1871 and 1911 maps reflect both the huge growth in population over the 19th century, and how families were often on the move: from just three counties the Spratlings have spread to 17, although Kent and Somerset remain the heartland.**

SPRATLING 1837-1847

SPRACKLEN 1841

DUNCTON 1841

This map again plots people with the surname Spratling, but this time in civil registration death records between 1837 and 1847 (ie 5 years either side of 1842 in the search box). The density in Somerset and Kent confirms the 1841 census results.

Another unusual surname, Spracklen, is believed to share its origins with Spratling (though there are different theories on the etymology). Here Somerset features again, with nearby Dorset the hotspot – could the Somerset Spratlings have branched off from them?

Looking at a surname that is rarer still can even confirm its etymology. One common type of surname is based on place names. A search in the 1841 census for the name 'Duncton' only shows results in Sussex – where the only village of that name in the UK is.

way of a centre point) to bring in more people. Also, you can look at births, marriages and deaths individually, which can yield further clues. For example, deaths will tend to reflect older people, so are slightly more likely to indicate where the family originally came from. Births may conversely indicate where the family has started up in a new area.

These are broad brush principles, of course – but if your ancestors have disappeared from civil or parish records, maps such as these might just jump-start your research again in a different part of the country.

Take a look at the various examples on these pages to see how powerful these tools can be. The census maps even work with keyword searches (ie without a surname), so you can track the growth or decline of a particular occupation, for example. To access the maps, use the site's Master Search feature, searching for a forename, surname or keywords. Then pick a census in the filters at the left-hand side: under each census year there is a link marked 'View a map of results'.

For the BMD maps, after performing your Master Search, select 'Births & Baptisms', 'Marriages' or 'Deaths and Burials' and click on the 'Map' link. Good luck with your plotting!

# Thinking outside the pox

*Every family would have been affected by smallpox.*
*Sue Wilkes explores the history of vaccination and the*
*marks it left in the archives*

Recent measles outbreaks have reignited the debate about the routine vaccination of children and parents' fears about possible adverse side-effects, but these issues are far from new. During Victorian times, some parents risked fines or even a prison sentence by refusing to allow their children to be vaccinated against smallpox.

Smallpox was a dreadful disease which killed thousands yearly; at one time around one in four people who caught the disease perished. Children were particularly vulnerable. Survivors were often left horribly disfigured by scars or even blind. In the early 18th century Lady Mary Wortley Montagu popularized the practice of inoculation ('variolation') in England. If a person was deliberately infected with smallpox through the skin, they caught a mild form of the disease, after which they were largely immune. However, some people died following inoculation.

In 1796 there was a major breakthrough: Dr Edward Jenner (1749–

**This 1802 cartoon by James Gillray, 'The Cow-Pock, or the Wonderful Effects of the New Inoculation!' mocks Edward Jenner for his pioneering vaccination work**

1823) published the results of his experiments on a boy named Phipps. Jenner showed that people inoculated with cow-pox (variolae vaccine) were mostly immune to smallpox. Cowpox was a milder disease than smallpox, so this was a less dangerous procedure.

Vaccination was very successful in combating the disease. As early as 1798, parish vestries such as Bozeat in Northamptonshire paid a physician to inoculate poor people in their parish (see W. E Tate, The Parish Chest (3rd edition), Cambridge University Press, 1979).

Following a horrific smallpox epidemic in 1837, an Act to Extend the Process of Vaccination (later amended) was passed in 1840. In England, Wales, and Ireland, Poor Law Boards of Guardians were given powers to use the poor rates to pay "medical officers or other practitioners for the

# VACCINATION RECORDS

Vaccination registers include details of each child's name, sex, date of birth, place where born, name and surname of father (or mother if the child was illegitimate), parent's profession, and the date of the medical certificate issued to confirm when the child was vaccinated. Vaccination officers' report books contain similar information.

Vaccination officers made 'Lists of Children' for whom they had not received certificates by the time they were four months old. These lists give each child's name, its number in the register of births, address, and the date when he/she was four months old. 'Returns of Deaths of Infants under Twelve Months of Age' (who had not been vaccinated) were also kept with vaccination registers. These returns give the child's number in the register of deaths, child's name, date and place of death, sex, age at death, name of father (mother if illegitimate), and parent's occupation.

Vaccination registers are subject to a closure period of at least 50 years from the date of the last entry in the ledger, but more usually 75 or 100 years, depending on the individual archive's policy. Access to registers of more recent date will be at the archivist's discretion; check that the record you wish to see is available before travelling.

Vaccination records can be found archived with poor law records or local health authority records (poor law boards were abolished in 1929). Check record office catalogues and TNA's Discovery (discovery.nationalarchives.gov.uk). Some locations are listed in Poor Law Union Records, Jeremy Gibson et al, (various editions, FFHS, 1997–2008).

Several archives have put transcripts of their vaccination registers online, or have listed the poor law unions for which registers are available. Some family history societies have published transcripts of the registers in print or on CD-ROM.

**Vaccination sources online**
- Registers held at Berkshire Archives (Berkshire FHS website): www.berksfhs.org.uk/berkshire/VaccinationRegisters.htm
- Registers held at Nottinghamshire Archives: http://cms.nottinghamshire.gov.uk/poor-lawrecords.pdf
- Vaccination registers for Wigan Poor Law Union 1899–1909: www.wlct.org/heritage-services/gwi155.pdf
- The Dr Jenner's House website has information on smallpox and vaccination history: www.jennermuseum.com

# IN THE REGISTERS

The Vaccination Register for Frodsham District (Runcorn Poor Law Union) for 1883–1885 shows that Mary Ann Farner, born 8 June 1883, daughter of John Farner, shoemaker of Top Lane, Kingsley, was vaccinated on 2 July 1883. John was issued with a certificate of successful vaccination on 16 October 1883 (Cheshire Archives and Local Studies, LGR3/7). Meanwhile the Wrenbury District (Nantwich Poor Law Union) 'Register of Births and Vaccinations' includes returns of infant deaths under one year old for 1877. Among the children listed are Raymond Martin Rogers of Oldham, who died age I year on 18 May 1877. His father was James Rogers, whose occupation was 'grocer' (CALS, LGN 2022/15/1).

gratuitous vaccination of all persons resident…" in their parish or union (Report on Small Pox and Vaccination in England and Wales, [434], 1853).

Vaccination was a public health measure, not 'relief' under the Poor Laws. After 1847 the Acts were administered by the Poor Law Board. However, the Vaccination Acts were 'permissive': Poor Law officials had no powers to enforce the law, and children were still at risk.

In 1853 an Act of Parliament made vaccination compulsory after Sir John Pakington reported that around 100,000 people caught smallpox annually in Great Britain and Ireland (Hansard's Parliamentary Debates, 3rd series, Vol. CXXIX, London, 1853). The 1853 Act required a parent or guardian to take their child to the local vaccination officer (appointed by the poor law board) before it was four months old. Vaccination was most effective if carried out at that age.

Some parents had fears about the vaccine (and there were cases when children had become ill after the procedure). The Anti-Compulsory Vaccination League was formed c.1867. Even some medical men who had personally vaccinated thousands of children, and were well aware of the vaccine's effectiveness, were against compulsory vaccination because they felt that it infringed civil liberties.

After 1871, vaccination officers worked in tandem with the registrars of births and deaths. Using information supplied by the registrars, officers compiled registers of successful vaccinations. Parents were given certificates of 'successful vaccination' or of 'postponed' vaccinations (if a child was poorly on the date scheduled for the procedure).

Even if vaccination registers have survived for your area of interest, you may not find an ancestor listed. Of the 891,000 children born in England and Wales in 1878, about 88,000 died before they could be vaccinated (roughly 10% of births). At the same date, around 4% of children born were missed because their parents moved and vaccination officers could not trace them.

In Dewsbury Poor Law Union alone, over 28% of children whose births had been registered were 'unaccounted for' (ie, unvaccinated) in the vaccination returns for 1873–1877, although by 1878 the proportion of defaulters had fallen to 13.5%. Other areas where the proportion of unprotected children was 10% or over included some London districts, and unions such as Banbury, Cheltenham and Burton-on-Trent, where the anti-vaccination movement had taken root. (Tenth Annual Report of the Local Government Board 1880-1881, [C.2982], (1881)).

Parents faced a 20s (£1) fine if their child was not vaccinated; non-payment could mean a prison sentence. Newspapers reported cases in the magistrates' courts. Check Quarter Sessions records for instances of parents' fines or penalties under the vaccination acts.

In 1898 a new 'conscience clause' allowed parents to 'opt out' of having their child vaccinated if a magistrate granted permission, and you may discover certificates of 'conscientious objection' against vaccination. The legislation was relaxed further in 1907, and vaccination rates declined.

**SUE WILKES** is the author of several books on social history and family history. Find out more about Sue's work at http://suewilkes.blogspot.com.

# RESEARCHING THE PROFESSIONALS

What if your ancestor was at the other end of the needle? Data website TheGenealogist has the largest collection of searchable occupational records online, available to Diamond subscribers. These records include an 1895 medical directory covering 'London, Provinces, Scotland and Ireland', where 'Provinces' means the rest of England and Wales.

This covers all known physicians, surgeons and general practitioners (plus licensed dental surgeons) at the time, with information about their qualifications and career history. It also lists medical colleges and provides details of current laws affecting the medical profession. As the image here shows, there are also fascinating advertisements for medical instruments of the time, including those used for vaccinations.

The book can be searched by name at **www.thegenealogist.co.uk/books/volume_index.php?rec_type=Medical**.

# Get your research on track

*From the mid-19th century onwards the railways employed many people in a wide variety of roles – many of their work records are going online*

In the late 19th century, more than a quarter of a million people were employed by the railway network, making it perfectly likely that you will have ancestors who worked in one of the many trades employed by the railway companies.

These people were not just stationmasters, porters and train drivers – there were of course many labourers extending the network sleeper by sleeper and maintaining the tracks. Also, there were accountants, architects, surveyors, clerks, inspectors, signalmen, gardeners and much more besides. In fact, almost 200 different railway-related occupations have been identified in staff records.

All of this is reflected in a huge and still-growing collection of railway employment records newly launched at data website TheGenealogist. The site began its railway collections with staff records from the Cornwall Railway – a triumph of engineering from Isambard Kingdom Brunel (with the Royal Albert Bridge across the River Tamar being the showpiece of the network) but a financial disaster zone which led to its absorption by the Great Western Railway only 40 years after the project had begun.

It has now added many more records, covering more than 50 counties across England and Wales and even the Isle of Man (which got its own railway network in the 1870s).

There are more than 1.3 million records available in the collection already, with many more in preparation – you can search them at **www.thegenealogist.co.uk/search/occupational/railway/**. Advanced

**The railway staff of Eastbourne Station pictured c1920**

search options include filtering by county, date of birth and keyword – the latter in particular is useful for narrowing down by job. The records typically also show where the person was based and can often be used to follow the progress of their career, especially when combined with research in the site's census records.

# A VICTORIAN RAILWAY DISASTER

One of the worst ever disasters faced by the Great Western Railway was the train crash at Shipton-on-Cherwell in Oxfordshire on Christmas Eve, 1874. A little north of Oxford the train's fireman James Hill spotted a passenger waving his hat out of the window of one of the third class carriages. The crew only identified what was wrong a mile or two later, by which time it was too late. The driver, Henry Richardson, spotted snow and dirt flying off the wheels of the same carriage as the train approached a wooden bridge over the River Cherwell and the Oxford Canal.

The London to Birmingham express was packed with people – as many as 500, according to the ticket records – and an extra, older carriage had been added at Oxford to help alleviate the pressure. This carriage had a broken tyre and, coupled with an inadequate braking system, it was crushed when the driver put on the brakes and the carriages behind derailed. A total of 34 people were killed and around 70 injured – a plaque at the bridge commemorates the disaster to this day.

An investigation by Colonel William Yolland of the Railway Inspectorate highlighted various safety problems and recommended an improved type of wheel to be fitted to trains in the future, as well as a new, telegraphic method of communicating between the engine and the rest of the train. Eventually automatic brakes were also fitted in the light of the knowledge gained from this crash.

A Mr C Day, who had been a passenger on the train, gave an eyewitness account of the aftermath of the accident: "We continued helping one and another until I was literally exhausted... Some help was obtained from the neighbourhood, but so little that they telegraphed to Birmingham, and a special train brought 100 labourers. Surgeons were also telegraphed for. One surgeon from the neighbourhood was most active, and used the splinters to set broken limbs, and tore up one lady's petticoat for bandages, and in the midst of his labour one fellow stole a watch and chain. They detected him, and he would have been lynched had not the police arrived in time, for broken telegraph wires were tied round his body and they were just going to drag him through the canal. The wires were broken by the carriages, which seemed as though they reared up in the air."

The unscrupulous thief he mentions is identified in newspaper reports as a 20-year-old gasfitter, Henry White, whose victim was solicitor Thomas Brown.

Several of the railway staff involved in the crash can be found in TheGenealogist's collection of railway staff records. Multiple records for individuals typically show different stages of their career. Henry Richardson appears twice, giving his year of birth as 1821. William Yolland is listed twice as a railway inspector based at Paddington, London (in 1877 he became the country's Chief Inspector of Railways). Another key figure listed is Frederick Bell, the stationmaster at nearby Kidlington. He saw the train rushing through, and later the first passenger running back down the track after the accident. Another inspector, Charles F Dodson, who was on the rescue train, is listed in the online records with date of birth 1820.

# Far from home

*Were your forebears among the British Home Children sent abroad? Emma Jolly explains how to trace them*

From 1869, child migrants known as 'Home Children' were sent via migrant organisations from Britain to its imperial dominions of Canada, South Africa, New Zealand and Australia. More than 150,000 orphaned or poverty-stricken children were sent to the settler colonies. Around 7,000 children were sent to Australia from Britain as part of the 'Home Children' emigration policy that lasted until 1967. The largest number of migrants – over 100,000 – was sent to Canada between 1869 and the early 1930s. This article explores how family historians can find out more about these child migrants, from their origins in the UK to their new lives in Canada.

One of the best resources to use when beginning research into child migrants is the database of around 20,000 British Home Children sent to Canada from 1869-1930 that can be explored at the Library and Archives Canada (LAC)'s website: **www.collectionscanada.gc.ca/databases/home-children/index-e.html**. This features a searchable index of immigration records, linking to images of passenger lists.

Also on this webpage is an index of Board of Guardians records. These need to be checked at the library itself, but online transcriptions give details of the sending agency, the name of the Board of Guardians that took the child into care and the year of arrival. These relate to Boards of Guardians in Britain, and more information may be found in archives in the UK (try the Access to Archives database **www.nationalarchives.gov.uk/a2a**).

Once you have established when your home child arrived in Canada, check the next census on which they should appear. Fortunately, the Canadian census is free to search at the LAC website – **www.bac-lac.gc.ca/eng/census/Pages/census.aspx** – but transcriptions of the 1851-1901 censuses can also be found easily on the Family Search website **www.familysearch.org**. The 1921 census is expected to be online very soon this year.

Later census records may indicate when your relative married. Follow this up in marriage records. A good source of marriage and death records is the Canadian Genealogy Center, **www.collectionscanada.gc.ca/genealogy/index-e.html**. Death and burial records should also be

# TRACING A BRITISH HOME CHILD

Bill Douglas of Ontario contacted me a few years ago to ask if I could help with the London origins of his grandfather, John Mills. John died a few days from his 90th birthday and had spoken often to Bill about his childhood. Bill knew that John's father was an alcoholic who abandoned the family. I was able to find the family on the 1891 census.

John married in London, during the World War One and his English marriage certificate revealed that John senior was a coppersmith. I found John's sister Marion's baptism record, which confirmed that their father was coppersmith, and I found the 1881 census entry which showed that the family temporarily moved to Kent. The census entries showed that John senior was born in Scotland and that his wife, Sarah, was from Sunderland. The names of the siblings matched those given as next of kin on John's war records.

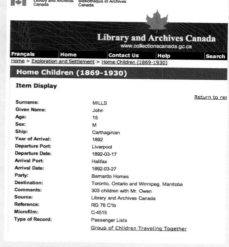

In Canada, Bill received help from Perry Snow and his website freepages.genealogy.rootsweb. ancestry.com/~britishhomechildren/ and Brian Gilchrist from the Brampton Central Library. John Mills is one of 57,000 Home Children named on Perry Snow's website in the British Home Children Registry.

This gives the full name of each child, their date or year of birth, their place of origin, the name of the ship on which they migrated, the year of migration, their age at migration and whether they are claimed or unclaimed by relatives.

The immigration records from Library and Archives Canada (LAC) revealed that John migrated in 1892 with Barnardo's, which took him in when the family fell into poverty.

Although there were a number of John Mills on the site, Bill remembered his grandfather telling him that he left England on St Patrick's Day from Liverpool. When Bill found a record of a John Mills who embarked on 17 March 1892, he knew it was his grandfather.

LAC's records mentioned 303 children arriving with 'Mr Owen'. More details on Alfred B Owen, Barnardo's Canadian Superintendent, were discovered at http://canadianbritishhome children.weebly.com/alfred-b-owen.html.

Also on the LAC site, Bill discovered via the 1901 census the farm family John was sent to and his war enlistment details in Toronto. This also revealed his date of birth as 14 June 1876, which tallied with family knowledge. From an online book by Wm. Perkins Bull, From Brock to Currie (at www.pinet.on.ca), Bill found that John was one a small number of Canadian soldiers who were selected to go to the Coronation of King George V. Page 351 of the book shows John in his military uniform (see above).

checked to confirm dates of birth, residences and names of next of kin. Check with local churches and cemeteries. Regional libraries may hold death notices for your relative or those named in military wills and other documents.

Many British Home Children volunteered to support their home country when Britain went to war against Germany in August 1914. Enlistment papers for soldiers, nurses and chaplains can be viewed for free and searched via the index on the LAC website: **www.collections-canada.gc.ca/databases/cef/index-e.html**. Those who lost their lives in the war should be recorded on the Commonwealth War Graves Commission's website at **www.cwgc.org**, although this remains incomplete.

Canadian records can tell you more about the institution or family to which your ancestor was sent. Most were sent to a 'receiving home'. In some cases, child migrants moved several times, and you may need to investigate more than one source in order to obtain the full picture. Receiving home organisations and agencies whose records are stored in Canada include the Children's Farm Home Association of London, England/ Elinore Home Farm of Nawigewauk, New Brunswick, Canada (c1903 to 1913) at Kings County Historical Society, Hampton, New Brunswick. St Catharine's Public Library, Ontario holds special collections on Home Children, including information on the Maria Rye Home at Niagara-on-the-Lake.

Family history societies also have useful resources. For example, the British Family History Society of Greater Ottawa's website, **www.bifhsgo.ca**, features an index for the Middlemore Homes. Pier 21 Museum in Nova Scotia has a dedicated section on Home Children at **www.pier21.ca/research/collections/the-story-collection/online-story-collection/british-home-children/**.

Records held in Britain can be used to establish the origins of Victorian and Edwardian children who were sent to Canada as part of this policy. These records can reveal details on the children's early homes and provide information on the families they left behind. In some cases, siblings were sent to Canada, either together or on separate journeys.

There are also confidential records, which may be retained by institutional archives in Britain or Canada. Often these are protected by privacy laws, which means they can only be accessed by close relatives of the child concerned. The largest of the sending agencies was the Barnardo Home for Boys whose records are held in England. Several smaller homes have given their case files to Barnardo's. An initial search of the archives for those whose relatives went to Canada or Australia is free of charge, but a fee will be required later to gain access to the full history. Full details are available at **www. barnardos.org.uk/what_we_do/who_we_are/history/family_history_ service/making_connections_form.htm**.

Another significant organisation was the Waif and Strays' Society. Its records can be obtained from its present incarnation, The Children's Society, at **www.childrenssociety.org.uk**. A digital archive of children in care, produced in conjunction with The Children's Society is online at **www.hiddenlives.org.uk**. This includes addresses and occupations of family members.

You may find more details of your ancestor and those he or she travelled with in outward passenger lists available online.

Using the details on these and on the Canada census returns, you should be able to find him or her on the Scottish, English and Welsh censuses. However, it is important to bear in mind that many Home Children lived for a period in institutions such as industrial schools or reformatories before they were sent to Canada. Thus they may be recorded on the census away from their family.

Where you are able to find the name of an institution where your ancestor lived in the UK, check the Access to Archives database to discover where surviving records, such as admission and discharge registers, are held. These should give useful genealogical details as well as address and personal facts.

Other resources to consult include local newspapers and magistrates reports, which may mention the parents or siblings of the Home Child in the context of crime, poverty or neglect.

**EMMA JOLLY** is a genealogist and writer. She has run the Genealogic research service (www. genealogic.co.uk) since 2006.

---

# MORE RESOURCES

- Perry Snow, Neither Waif Nor Stray: The Search for a Stolen Identity (Universal Publishers, 2000)
- Phyllis Harrison (ed), The Home Children (J Gordon Shillingford Publishing, 2003)
- Gail H Corbett, Nation Builders: Barnardo Children in Canada (Dundurn Group, 2002)

Lists of various Canadian Home Children websites and contact information in both Canada and Britain can be found at http://jubilation.uwaterloo.ca/~marj/genealogy/children/ tracers.html. A list of contacts for records held in the UK is on the Barnardo's website at http://www.barnardos.org.uk/canada-5.pdf.

# Lucky dip

*A large and eclectic collection of name-based data has gone online – is your ancestor in there?*

Family history is of course a discipline, requiring proper research skills and methodologies to be learned and a knowledge of specific archives to be learned over time. The fact remains, though, that sometimes it's serendipity which can advance our research when a brick wall seems insurmountable.

Online at data giant TheGenealogist is an extensive and diverse collection of almost 37,000 names which offers something of a lucky dip to family historians. The TNA Names collection (previously known as PRO Names and only available as three separate indexes on CD) brings together a wide range of references to personal names found across many different series of records held at The National Archives (TNA) in Kew, London. It was originally compiled by the researcher Stuart Tamblin between 1997 and 1999 and is now online, fully searchable at **www.thegenealogist.co.uk/search/miscellaneous/tna/**. Many of the records are military in origin – but by no means all.

The first of the three original indexes which form this collection had more than 13,000 entries, around 50% relating to the Royal Navy and Royal Marines, with a further 30% having their source in the Army or Royal Air Force; around 5% of these records relate to criminals such as smugglers.

The second set, again around 13,000 records, was also dominated by the Navy and Marines, but a quarter of the records this time related to criminals. In addition there were around 1000 records relating to policemen. Another 10,000 records formed a third index following a similar pattern to the others.

In total almost 40 different series of records at The National Archives are represented in this data. The military collections include muster rolls or crew lists of particular vessels such HMS Neptune in 1805 (and even HMS Bounty from 1787), casualty lists, court martials and medal rolls, plus a list of soldiers executed between 1914 and 1920. Other collections represented include hospital registers, 'criminal lunatics' from Bethlehem Hospital and other asylums in the 19th century and smaller collections as diverse as Cheshire jurors from 1813 to records of the Liverpool Necropolis Burial Ground.

The time span is also wide: the earliest records in the combined collection date from 1604 and the most recent from 1995 (making due allowance for Data Protection legislation).

TheGenealogist's easy to use interface allows the data to be searched by name, rank (where appropriate) and year, with advanced options for service/organisation and military unit. The results that are returned then include the TNA series reference for tracking down the original documents at Kew – these may include more information, of course. These references are conveniently hyperlinked directly to TNA's new Discovery catalogue system.

As Mr Tamblin wrote with the original collection, "This index should be looked upon as a pointer to original records, indicating which classes might fruitfully be searched once you have found a name of interest."

Overall this collection forms a rich treasure trove in which you might just find that elusive piece of information needed for exploring an ancestor's life further, especially if they had military or criminal connections.

# FOUND IN TNA NAMES

As an example, if we search for an Albert Brice, this collection brings up Albert Bertram Brice, who served on HMS Shark in 1916. Clicking the TNA reference (ADM 104/146) pinpoints him in a register of the killed and wounded.

We can also look up at TheGenealogist's Master Search to make connections with other records. A roll of honour confirms he died in the Battle of Jutland at the age of 21, and gives his parents' names, which can be used to track the family back in census and civil registration records at the site.

# Find ships' crews online

*If you have ancestors who set sail with the Navy or merchant fleets in the 19th century, an online resource could help you*

The 19th century saw a major transformation for Britain's navy and shipping industries alike. After the Napoleonic wars, the 'Pax Britannica' saw Britain reign supreme as the leading global maritime power. Although there were no major sea battles between 1827 (the Battle of Navarino in the Greek War of Independence) and World War One, the Navy itself underwent a sea-change from wood and sail to steam and steel.

Powered by the Industrial Revolution, the merchant navy likewise was tranformed by technology, and saw worldwide dominance in line with the strength of the British Empire. In the 1830s, regular steamship voyages began across the Atlantic, aiding trade and of course taking many of our ancestors between the old world and the new. The lucrative trade in sugar, tea and spices provided much of the economic power behind Britain's supremacy.

Thus many of us will have forebears who took to the sea during the 19th and early 20th centuries, whether in the Royal Navy or in merchant ships, let alone the ongoing fishing industry.

Although merchant seamen were obliged to be registered from 1835, central registration petered out in 1857 and was only reinstated in 1914. It can therefore be complicated to trace the maritime career path of ancestors in this period.

Fast-growing data website **TheGenealogist.co.uk** offers an important new resource for those with seafaring ancestors. It gives details of more than 439,000 Royal Navy and merchant seamen's records, which are searchable by name, rank, age and ship. The full crew list can be displayed for any of the ships.

# RULING THE WAVES

One example available at TheGenealogist's new crew lists collection is the large crew of the training vessel HMS Britannia, which was docked in Dartmouth. She used to be the magnificent HMS Prince of Wales with 121 guns and was one of six first-rate three-decker line of battleships. Launched in 1860 she was renamed HMS Britannia in 1869 and was then used for cadet training.

Searching for Captain Noel Digby in the advanced search brings up his details out of all the records and allows his full record to be displayed. The Britannia's full crew list can also be shown along with the original image of the record.

Digby was born in 1839 - his crew record shows his birthplace as Dorset - and he enrolled with the Navy in November 1852, ultimately reaching the rank of Vice Admiral. His service record is available online at The National Archives website (http://discovery.nationalarchives.gov.uk/SearchUI/Details?uri=D7587698).

Covering the years 1851-1911, these include lists and agreements for those involved in merchant shipping and ships' crews for those at home ports, at sea and abroad.

Details given may include age, place of birth, rank and ticket number, previous and current ships with ports of registration, dates and places of joining and leaving, and reason for leaving.

The records are from a variety of sources which include The National Archives series BT 98 and specialist county and non-county census records such as those to be found in series RG 9 and RG 10.

The BT 98 lists and agreements are intended to find many of those involved in merchant shipping who cannot be located on the 1851 census because they simply were not at home to be enumerated. Some were at ports in the British Isles many miles from home and some were not even in the country.

The later census-related records include lists for naval personnel on board merchant and Royal Navy vessels, around the UK and abroad.

As an example from BT 98, searching for David Benzie shows us the two ships he was master of during 1851 – the Brothers of Aberdeen and the Prospect of Aberdeen – and then by clicking on the full details icon the site reveals his information, including his ticket number, when he joined and left, and his previous vessel (Betsy of Aberdeen). A third record for Benzie, this time from RG 9, shows him as master of the

Sophia in Sunderland. In this case a scan of the original census image is also available.

This one example shows the power of this data set – although many crew records can already be found in census collections, it is hard to make the connections for the same individual over time. Here we have found a sizeable chunk of one man's seagoing career in a matter of seconds.

The full crew list for each ship can be also viewed by clicking on the ship icon next to the search results. An advanced search is also available where you can use the ship's name.

This record set can be found under TheGenealogist's occupational records collection – these records are available for those with a Diamond subscription.

Other linked records of interest include the large collection of Navy Lists under military rolls and lists at the site.

# Something for everyone

*Mairead Mahon explores the history of department stores*

D
epartment stores have been in existence for almost 200 years and quite often they have reflected huge social and technological changes.

Long before the birth of the department store, people have always shopped. In medieval times, this was done at weekly markets, the forerunners of our market towns. As the centuries passed, simple shops, consisting of a board outside living premises with unglazed windows, began to appear. Traders would sell only one type of product and usually groups of them such as butchers would sell their wares in the same area.

In the 18th century, some shops began to become grander establishments. A more leisured class, with time and money, appeared and luxury goods became more affordable. The relief on glazing tax meant that goods could be displayed behind elegant windows and items such as fine silks and delicate china were displayed in spacious show or ware rooms.

House of Fraser Archives, Glasgow University Archive Services

**Derry and Toms department store in London, 1937. The company was founded in the 1860s by Joseph Toms and Charles Derry. The building in Kensington High Street is now used by various retailers**

# WINDOW DISPLAYS

Department stores have always realised the importance of display and the availability of huge plate glass windows enabled this. Owners believed The Draper's Record's comment that business was done "between the public and the shop window".

The arrival of lifelike mannequins in the early 20th century helped, although police had to be called to one Scottish store when people mistook mannequins with moving eyes and chests for human beings. Harrods advertised its sale by displaying an elephant made entirely out of white towels and Lewis's in Liverpool advertised its new range of Harris tweeds by constructing a life size crofter's cottage in the window.

It was Gordon Selfridge, though, who gained the reputation of King of the Windows, although even he caused amazement when he managed to display Amy Johnson's airplane. Unfortunately, his signature window, inscribed with signatures of stars that visited the store, was damaged in World War Two.

Shopping was becoming a pleasurable experience for an expanding middle class whose sense of style was expressing itself in fashion and furnishings. More and more people became shopkeepers in order to capitalise on this new consumer demand for luxury goods: it was hardly a surprise when Napoleon referred to England as "a nation of shopkeepers".

But it was the Industrial Revolution which led to dramatic changes in the way our ancestors shopped. An increase in urban populations and the coming of the railways meant that shops had more to sell and more people to sell to. Many of these people had money to spend on the new goods that were coming in from all around the world and the first retailers to see the potential of the situation were the drapers.

In the 19th century fashion was becoming very big business, with a young, beautifully dressed Queen on the throne and a newly burgeoning magazine market began to tell ladies how to be fashionable. It wasn't just dresses or material that ladies needed to emulate the look: they had to have accessories such as gloves, stockings, bags and parasols, and the draper began to expand his stock so that all these things could be found under one roof. They were, as the historian Sir Roy Strong says, "the proto-department store" and as time passed, the shops had to become bigger than ever before to accommodate all their wares.

There were many examples of this. Kendal, Milne and Faulkner in Manchester is just one, which today belongs to House of Fraser. In 1836, it was a simple draper's store but in the space of ten years, it was supplying everything a lady could require, as well as offering services as diverse as upholstery and funeral undertaking.

Like many others of its type, it also fixed prices and introduced a ready money payment scheme, declining to give credit to all except its most valued customers. Customers would hand their money to an assistant who would put it in a tube and send it along a wire to a cashier, who would write out a receipt and return it with any change. This system, known as the 'cash railway', was a very popular and is still in use today in Jacksons of Reading.

Department stores gained a reputation as places where shopping could be a truly pleasurable experience. Early stores often grew haphazardly but as they became more prosperous these were often knocked down and splendid new purpose-built stores were constructed. These contained everything for the comfort of the customer: tea rooms, smoking rooms for gentlemen, electric light, spacious shop floors and, quite often, musicians to entertain as one browsed. Department stores were keen to afford their customers the latest innovations. Harrods, for example, installed the first ever escalator in a British store in 1898. It was a mixed success, however, as customers were quite often so shaken after

# DEPARTMENT STORE ARCHIVES

Many department stores have archives which can be consulted by those who are either interested in their history or by those who think that an ancestor may have worked in one and would like to glean some information about them.

Archives contain a fascinating collection of historical documents, which reflect our changing consumer tastes and give a valuable insight into what it was like to work and shop in department stores. These documents include material such as photographs, advertisements, catalogues, minutes of meetings and general employment rules.

Staff magazines also feature in many archives and these often contain accounts of staff outings, Christmas parties and material relating to individuals such as marriages, retirements and obituaries. Some stores, for example Marks and Spencer plc, also produced special staff magazines for colleagues who fought in the war and several maintain rolls of honour for those who fell. These can be very useful in tracing individuals.

It is important to realise that smaller stores may have been incorporated into larger groups and if so, the first thing to do is to check which group it was incorporated into and then consult their archives. In cases where the store went out of business, The National Archives may be able to help with locating any available records.

Stores such as The House of Fraser and Marks and Spencer plc have accessible archives which are open to the public and professional archivists who are willing to help trace a particular ancestor.

**Some useful web addresses:**
- www.housefraserarchive.ac.uk
- marksintime.marksandspencer.com
- archiveshub.ac.uk/search/search.html – a search for 'department store' reveals many further such archives
- There is an online museum of North American department stores at departmentstoremuseum.blogspot.com

using it that smelling salts and brandy would be offered to them!

Many stores were proud of their huge range of stock and one store, Whitley's – dubbed 'the Universal Provider' – vowed that it could supply anything from a pin to an elephant. Sumptuous catalogues were provided, so that customers could browse goods at home and stores even had their own horse-drawn transport and, later, vans to deliver their order, sometimes the same day.

The very size of department stores meant that they became a large employer. Jobs covered the whole spectrum and included managerial staff, buyers, bookkeepers, cafe staff, porters and cleaners. However, the people that the public had most contact with were the shop floor workers. There was a strict hierarchy from department head to the most junior assistant. Very often, the whole of the shop floor was overseen by a floor walker, usually a man, who would ensure the smooth day-to-day running of the store and occasionally act as a discreet security guard.

Many assistants worked a 60-hour week. Most lived in and board and lodging was included in their salary, a situation which resembled a fairly strict boarding school. Emily Faithful, writing in 1864, considered that it was good clean employment for girls. However, she also suggested that they would need "the power of standing for many hours" and "entire self control" when dealing with rude customers. Handbooks of rules were issued, which generally listed the huge amount of failings which would result in fines: anything from talking to wrapping a customer's parcel badly. However, conditions were eased in 1909, with a bill forbidding excessive hours and gradually the draconian rules were also relaxed leading many department stores to forge reputations as excellent employers.

The history of department stores is a rich and huge area. It can tell us much about the consumer habits of our ancestors, who loved shopping enough to make them a reality.

**MAIREAD MAHON** has an MA in Victorian History and her speciality is writing about social history. She has broadcast on national and local radio and gives talks throughout the north west of England.

# School records

*Kirsty Gray offers an education in exploring our ancestors'
childhoods through records from schooldays*

Two hundred years ago, education, which we take for granted today, was a commodity only guaranteed for nobility and the rich. Before the 20th century, relatively few people needed to be able to read or write, since there were plenty of jobs that did not need literacy and numeracy. It was up to individuals to arrange for their children's education and there were a variety of different ways to deliver it. Reforms in the 19th century brought education to the masses and schools were founded for the poor, including elementary schools, 'ragged' schools and district schools with many Roman Catholic, Methodist and Baptist schools proliferating.

Records of your ancestors' schooldays can provide a rare glimpse of

## ATTENDANCE RECORDS

The log book for Peter Tavy National School in October 1898, pictured here, records many events which affect the attendance of the scholars including the local Tavistock Goose Fair and parents being summoned for 'irregularity' in their children's attendance. The head teacher at Chilsworthy School writes, on 16 December 1930, "Harold Sillifant sent home at 1 o'clock accompanied by brother, Willie – having badly cut his head while playing" and an entry in the Holsworthy Wesleyan School log book in 1890 gives an indication of some of the reasons why children stayed away from their desks:

*The following are those who, for various reasons, have not attended school regularly during the year 1889/90:*

*F. Badcock – Delicate Health*
*W. Rees – Sickness*
*J. Ford – Employed*
*T. Wicks – Sickness of Sister*
*W. Sillifant – Liking for Wildlife*

The record below from 20 May 1878 shows two new scholars at Pancrasweek School, Emily Gilbert, aged 6 (born 3 December 1871) and William Sillifant, aged 4 (born 10 May 1874). William progressed from Standard I to Standard IV, leaving the school in 1887 at the age of 13 while Emily only remained at the school until she was 10, with no recorded progress in the admission register.

their childhood. What school did they attend? How long did they attend for? How did they perform at school? You may find clues in original school records or printed registers, many of which survive from the 19th century and some even date back to medieval times.

School attendance to the age of ten was only made compulsory in 1870 and secondary schooling remained dominated by public (fee-paying) and grammar schools (although these accepted a few poor children by way of scholarships). From 1862, all schools had to keep log books, written up in great detail by head teachers. These books recorded visitors to the school, inspections, holidays, staff changes, attendance, student awards and events of local significance.

Admission registers were mostly kept after 1870. In the front of the register, the masters and mistresses from the commencement of the school are noted and the admission records for the scholars contain a wealth of detail including date of admission, date of birth, name of parent/guardian, their academic progress, the school they came from and where they went on to attend (if applicable). The 'remarks' column available in some registers often contains fascinating snippets such as 'left for service', 'left the district', 'wanted at home', 'dead', 'apprenticed

# SCHOOL REGISTERS ONLINE

Many school registers are becoming available online. TheGenealogist.co.uk has education registers from 30 areas of England and Scotland. These include famous private establishments such as Eton, Uppingham, Marlborough College and the Loretto School in Edinburgh. In some cases there are brief biographical details with information about parents and sponsors.

This collection is by no means only for people with wealthy ancestors, however. Also included, for example, are registers from grammar schools in Carlisle, Bury St Edmunds and Leeds (the images here are of Leeds Free Grammar School and its records).

The collection also includes several university registers,

for example from Aberdeen, Cambridge, Oxford and Glasgow, which might help follow an ancestor into further education. All of these records are accessible via the site's Master Search, or to browse through the School, College and University Registers collection.

Astonishingly some of the records date back as far as the early 13th century. At the time of writing the most recent records are from 1949.

to...' and many other notes providing an insight into the lives of our forebears after leaving education.

Other school records may include attendance registers, class lists, punishment books, honours books and accident books, revealing further details of an ancestor's school life.

If you know the name of the school, you may find it is still there and in possession of its own archives. Alternatively, the records may be deposited in the local studies library, county record office or, in the case of church schools, in the denomination's archives. You can work out where your ancestor may have been educated by consulting contemporary directories.

Church of England school records may be located among other parish papers, while workhouse school records will be held with those of poor law unions. Family papers may often contain school reports, team photographs and leaving certificates.

Access to Archives (**http://www.nationalarchives.gov.uk/a2a**) is an excellent online resource providing the facility to search and browse for information about collections of records, cared for in local record offices and libraries, universities, museums and national and specialist institutions across England and Wales, where they are made available to the public. A quick search for 'school' and 'Cornwall', for example, provides 8,220 hits of which 7,794 documents are held at Cornwall Record Office.

**KIRSTY GRAY** holds many roles from Chairman of the Guild of One-Name Studies to Director of English Studies for the National Institute for Genealogical Studies, as well as being director of her own professional research business.

# Lost way of life

*Nell Darby explores a forgotten corner of London's history*

*"We all work nets alike up and down the river – we have been brought up to fishing."* – Joseph Armitage, 1830

It's hard to imagine it today, but in the 18th and 19th centuries the London suburbs of Hammersmith and Chiswick were fishing villages. Working on the river had been a major feature of life in London since medieval times, and for many years, St Nicholas' church in Chiswick, situated on the riverbank near the old Thames ferry crossing, was known as the fishermen's church, named after the patron saint of sailors and fishermen. Local fishermen plundered the Thames for its stocks of salmon, eels, flounder and smelt, often being taught by their fathers from a young age, and eventually taking over their nets and boats.

Chiswick and Hammersmith were once seen as healthy, rural villages and by the late 18th century were attracting affluent city dwellers, who built grand houses in the area. On the surface, fishing life continued as

**Peter boats on the Thames – these allegedly had their origins in boats used to ferry passengers to and from St Peter's Abbey, the Saxon predecessor to Westminster Abbey in London. By early modern times, a Peter boat was a double ended fishing boat of about 12 feet in length**

# AN INDUSTRY IN DECLINE

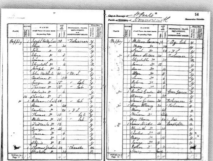

The gradual decline of the fishing industry in Chiswick and Hammersmith can be followed through the collection of censuses available at **www.thegenealogist.co.uk**.

If you search for the two keywords 'fisherman Chiswick', for example, using the site's powerful Master Search feature, there are 21 results – note that to search without a surname in this way you must specify a year or a county (here Middlesex). In 1851 the equivalent figure is only 6.

In 1851 Joseph Wakeman was one of the relatively few Chiswick-born fishermen still living and working in the area. Aged 61, he was working with his son, 19-year-old Joseph, and had a fishmonger living next door, but other neighbours worked in non-fishing related industries, as shown here.

The censuses also reveal that the brother of Moses Gibson (see main article), Lewis, though, had to relocate to Putney to fish –

**[MIDDLESEX.]** FIS

**FISHMONGERS.**

Andrew W., Harrow-on-the-Hill
Atkins J. jun. High street, Highgate
Barnet E. High street, Uxbridge
Batterham W. Boston lane, Hanwell
Bilton J. Silver street, Enfield
Bilton B. Powder's cut, Enfield
Bivand T. Church terrace, Ealing
Bolland J. New road, Hammersmith
Booter Mrs. F. Church street, Hackney
Bottoms S. Great Stanmore
Brode W. Church street, Hackney
Brown J. Devonshire road, Chiswick
Brown T. Halfacre, Old Brentford
Clark J. Sunbury
Clark W. King st. east, Hammersmith
Cole J. 5 Baker's buildings, St. Matthias road, Stoke Newington
Constable T. High street, Highgate
Cottrell M. 13 Broadway, London fields, Hackney
Crowther T. J. High street, Homerton
Dimmock T. Hanwell
Ellis C. London street, Uxbridge
Evans J. High street, Fulham
Fermor A. J. Church row, Tottenham
Garner S. London road, Twickenham
Gibson W. T. & G. King William place, West end, Hammersmith
Godley J. 7 Cotton row, Marlborough road, Dalston
Golbourn S. Hackney wick
Hall C. King st. west, Hammersmith
Hallett S. H. Church street, Hackney
Harris B. Church street, Twickenham
Harris G. King street, Twickenham
Harrison J. High street, Hounslow
Heaps J. 5 West st. Triangle, Hackney
Heyburn W. Pinner, Watford
Horne J. High road, Tottenham
Hunt W. High st. Stoke Newington
Hurlock J. 5 Caledonia place, Well street, Hackney
Jeaper Thomas, Southgate
Johnson N. 21 High st. Stoke Newington

he is listed in the 1851 census with his family at 5 Spring Gardens; Moses himself became a fishmonger, shown in 1851 at 4 King William Street, Hammersmith.

This new trade in the family is confirmed in an 1862 Post Office directory for Middlesex (left), where a branch of the Gibsons is now listed as fishmongers in Hammersmith. An introductory section on the parish of Chiswick in the same directory makes no mention of fishing itself as a trade in the area, and there are no fishermen listed as such in the trade section.

---

it always had – with some fun interspersed with the hard work. In 1829, 23-year-old Moses Gibson, whose grandfather, father and brothers were all fishermen, had taken part in an annual sailing match between 24 boats, all owned by fishermen. In a test of skill, they had to sail their boats from Hammersmith Bridge to Kew and back. The local gentry and other well-to-do residents donated monetary prizes, and turned out to watch the race. Moses came second in his boat, the Countess Macartney, narrowly losing out to Thomas Humphreys in his boat, the Providence. These were both Peter boats – traditional, double-ended fishing boats designed to deal with the Thames' tidal waters.

But there was, underneath this jollity, increasing pressure on the fishing industry and those who worked in it. Pollution caused by industrialisation was leading to a dearth of fish and therefore less income for the fishermen. One's equipment – nets and so on – cost a substantial amount of money, and others might try and steal them to use themselves or sell on.

Moses Gibson was the victim of such a theft in 1830. At the Old Bailey, he accused two brothers, William and Joseph Armitage, of stealing his fishing nets, worth about two shillings, from his new boat, the Godspeed, while it was docked in its usual place outside Hammersmith's Old Ship pub. The local fishing community all knew each other; as Moses stated in court, "I know the prisoners - they are fishermen, but seldom work on the river Thames." Another fisherman, William Pearce, had seen William Armitage with two nets, and recognised them as "my brother's nets".

The fishermen who shared this stretch of the Thames usually saw each other as brothers, and would protect each other. Joseph, aged 21, and his brother William, 20, were both sentenced to 14 years' transportation to Australia for the theft.

By 1839, writer Thomas Faulkner was lamenting the state of the fishing industry in Hammersmith, saying that so few smelt fish had appeared in the area during the previous five years "that the produce scarcely pays the fishermen for their labour in catching them". Apart from the likes of the Armitage brothers, local fishermen formed a tight community, supporting each other when times were hard. When William Pearce, a Chiswick fisherman, was called to the Brentford Petty Sessions to answer a charge of infringing the fishery rules in 1839, the magistrates' room

# FURTHER INFORMATION

St Nicholas' Church in Chiswick still holds the complete registers of baptisms, marriages and burials from 1678 to the present day. The church's archive group can be contacted at Archivists, c/o St Nicholas Parish Office, The Vicarage, Church Street, Chiswick, W4 2PJ.

The local website for Chiswick, www.chiswickw4.com, has a wealth of local history information.

Brentford and Chiswick Local History Society (www.brentfordandchiswicklhs.org.uk) has a well-designed index to local people, crimes, industries, places and much more.

The Fulham and Hammersmith Historical Society (www.fhhs.wordpress.com) has a more basic website, but includes links and contact information.

The Hammersmith and Fulham Archives are administered by the City of Westminster Archives Centre, and is open on Mondays only, 10am-4pm, by appointment only. Contact archives@westminster.gov.uk or call 020 7641 5180 (www.lbhf.gov.uk/Directory/Leisure_and_Culture/Libraries/Archives/17430_Archives_and_Local_History.asp).

was crowded with other fishermen there to support one of their brothers. William, however, was found guilty, fined 50 shillings and sent to the house of correction for a month. His brother John then received the same penalty, and also had his valuable net, worth £7, confiscated.

As time went on many local fishermen, under pressure from the decreasing numbers of fish and increased pollution, continued to fight against the regulations governing fishing. In September 1854, Moses and Lewis Gibson's other brother, James, together with fellow Hammersmith fishermen James Holder and John Gibbs, were charged with obstructing two water-bailiffs after they were caught using an illegal net on the river at Richmond. They were convicted, and fined £1 each.

By the late 1860s, Chiswick and Hammersmith were no longer fishing villages but bustling London suburbs, workers shunning the river for other jobs in the city. An 1868 gazetteer described Hammersmith as a "suburban district", and stressed its brickfields, iron-foundry and forge, wax-bleaching grounds and breweries rather than its fishing community. Likewise, in the 1870s, Chiswick was noted in another gazetteer for its gas-works and sewage system. It was clear that a way of life that had existed for centuries was virtually over.

**NELL DARBY** (www.nelldarby.com) is a freelance writer, specialising in social history and the history of crime. She has a PhD in gender and the summary process in the 18th century.

# Light industry

*Picture historian Jayne Shrimpton puts the lives of photographer ancestors in focus and explains and how to trace them*

Early in 1839 the wonderful invention of photography was officially announced to the world. Soon its commercial potential was becoming realised and a new occupation was emerging – that of the professional studio photographer. The first photographic rooms offering luxury daguerreotype portraits opened during the 1840s. In the following decades, as photographic techniques advanced, prices reduced and demand for portrait photographs extended throughout society, and the number of commercial studios soared. In the 1851 census 51 professional photographers were recorded operating throughout Britain; by 1861 there were almost 3,000 and in 1871 more than 4,700. These figures continued to grow until the 1910s: then professional portrait photography reached its height before beginning a slow decline, reflecting the rise of amateur photography.

Studio photography was an attractive proposition: the trade was open to virtually anyone and potentially it could generate a decent income. In particular, the surge in public demand for carte de visite 'album portraits' during the early 1860s encouraged many to try their hand at commercial photography. Combining science and art, the practice of photography naturally appealed to opticians, chemists, watchmaker/jewellers, artists, printers, frame-makers and the like, but also attracted diverse tradesmen and entrepreneurs, from boot makers to bakers.

Some photographers ran a studio as a sideline alongside their main craft or trade, often from a room in their home or shop, while others operated as full-time photographers, renting town-centre premises and employing assistants. Professional photography was a competitive industry but those

**This self-portrait with photographic equipment was taken by photographer Hermann Krone in 1858**

# PHOTOGRAPHERS RESEARCH GUIDE

The activities of some past photographers are already well-recorded, while relatively little is known about others. Family historians may occasionally need to conduct primary research using census returns and trade publications, although the chances are that an individual or organisation – perhaps a local history society, photograph collector or family historian investigating old family photographs – has already noted their existence. If your ancestor was an eminent society photographer then they will probably be represented in the Photographs Collection at the National Portrait Gallery, London. See the NPG website for photographer listings: www.npg.org.uk/collections/about/photographs-collection/photographers-represented-in-the-collection.php

Similarly, it may be possible to discover more about a named photographer who ran a successful neighbourhood business by contacting the local museum, record office or archive for the relevant area.

As with many aspects of genealogical research, much basic information is now available online. There isn't a comprehensive national directory of nineteenth- and early twentieth-century photographers, but a general internet search for your ancestor's name (and address, if known) may lead to one of the searchable photography websites or A-Z indexes that have been compiled for some geographical regions and uploaded onto the internet. These free resources vary in their scope and content: most list photographer names, studio addresses and their recorded operational dates while some also include detailed biographies of named photographers and may even display examples of their work. The main regional photographer databases currently available to view for free are listed below:

**Bristol:** Bristol Photographers 1852-1972, http://www.rogerco.pwp.blueyonder.co.uk/search/bristolphotographers.htm
**Cambridgeshire, Huntingdonshire, Leicestershire, Norfolk, Northamptonshire, Rutland and Suffolk:** Early Photographic Studios: A-Z directories of photographers in Cambridgeshire etc www.early-photographers.org.uk
**Channel Islands:** Jersey Photographers and Studios www.jerseyfamilyhistory.co.uk
**Derbyshire:** Photographers & Photographic Studios in Derbyshire, www.genealogy.rootsweb.ancestry.com/~brett/photos/dbyphotos.html
**Hampshire:** Isle of Wight Photographers c.1840-1940 www.iowphotos.info/

**London:** Database of 19th Century Photographers & Allied Trades, 1841-1901, www.photolondon.org.uk
**Scotland:** History of Photography in Edinburgh, www.edinphoto.org.uk; Glasgow's Victorian Photographers, www.thelows.madasafish.com/main.htm
**Sussex:** Sussex Photo History, www.photohistory-sussex.co.uk/index.htm; Directory of Photographic Studios in Brighton & Hove 1841-1910, www.spartacus.schoolnet.co.uk/Brighton-Photographers.htm
**Wales:** Victorian Professional Photographers in Wales, 1850-1925, www.genuki.org.uk/big/wal/VicPhoto1.html
**Warwickshire:** Victorian Photography Studios...in and around Birmingham and Warwickshire www.hunimex.com/warwick/photogs.html

If details of a named photographer ancestor cannot be accessed online, then visiting the website Photographers of Great Britain and Ireland, 1840-1940 is highly recommended: www.cartedevisite.co.uk. This helpful resource focuses on commercial studio photographers and their customers. Accurate studio data is available for over 62,000 named photographers, for a modest fee. The website operator, Ron Cosens – who has written for both printed editions of Discover Your Ancestors – also welcomes communication from family historians investigating photographer ancestors and will work with them to produce a biography and detailed business history. Completed photographer biographies have been uploaded onto the site: http://www.cartedevisite.co.uk/photographers-category/biographies/

Additionally, information about photographers operating in some cities or counties has been published in printed publications. A comprehensive list of titles is included in Robert Pols's book, below. The following books are also useful for understanding the work of a studio photographer.

• My Ancestor was a Studio Photographer by Robert Pols (Society of Genealogists, 2011).
• Victorian Photographers at Work by John Hannavy (Shire, 1997)
• The Victorians: Photographic Portraits by Audrey Linkman (Tauris Parke, 1993)

# AN OXFORD BUSINESS

Online investigations into a possible distant ancestor, Thomas Shrimpton, Oxford studio photographer, revealed no convenient photographer database covering the city, or county of Oxfordshire. However the website www.cartedevisite.co.uk supplied data (deriving from census returns and trade advertisements) for a small fee, confirming that the business entitled Thos Shrimpton & Son, as printed on the mount featured here, operated from 23/24 Broad Street, Oxford between 1871 and 1902. Further online searches also turned up a website dedicated to Broad Street, Oxford, which displays a modern photograph of the handsome Georgian building that was their studio (now part of Blackwell's Music Shop). It also states that on earlier censuses Thomas and his son had been recorded as booksellers, print sellers and publishers at that address: www.headington.org.uk/oxon/broad/buildings/south/23,24,25.htm.

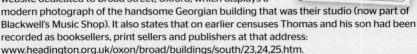

The original census records for 1851-1901 need to be checked, but it seems possible that Thomas and Alfred Shrimpton continued with their complementary trade after they took up studio photography.

who succeeded often remained in business for decades, perhaps taking on new working partners, expanding into larger premises or opening new branches, and eventually handed over a thriving business to their sons.

Commercial photography was a male-dominated arena, but independent female photographers did exist, while other women assisted photographer fathers, husbands and brothers in the studio, or worked as colourists, re-touching black and white photographs. Far more people were employed in the industry than census statistics suggest, yet tens of thousands of named photographers were recorded between the mid-19th and mid-20th centuries and many family historians today can claim descent from the commercial photographers of the past.

The historical evidence available for researching photographer ancestors mainly concerns the professional operators who worked under their own name: it can be impossible to trace the junior photographers and anonymous assistants who worked behind the scenes within a commercial studio. Original sources of information about identified photographers may be found in the decennial census returns, business advertisements in local newspapers and trade directories and extant photographs bearing their name and studio details, although minor operators and those who dipped in and out of the trade may not have been included on census returns and probably advertised only rarely, if at all: these have left little trace of their activities, except perhaps for random photographs taken at their studio.

Few of our ancestors left behind tangible evidence of their occupation, trade or skill, yet the professional output of numerous studio photographers survives today in the form of privately- or publicly-owned photographs printed with their business name and address. Sometimes photographs originating in the studio of a photographer ancestor have been handed down the generations as family heirlooms but, if not, examples of his or her work may be found illustrated in books, displayed on the internet, or preserved within local library, museum or archive collections. It may even be possible to buy some of their photographs from private dealers or sellers on eBay or other commercial sites. It is very rewarding to be able to study, even hold in the hand, the physical products of forebears' expertise or, at least, pictures created under their direct supervision.

Photographic mounts are also akin to trade cards and sometimes the backs of the cards display interesting information about their business, alongside the photographer/studio name and address(es) . Keen to publicise any features likely to impress clients, photographers sometimes included on their mounts mention of any photographic awards or medals won; royal warrants if they were patronised by royalty; brief descriptions of their facilities; itemised prices of their products; and details of their services, for example whether they were able to make home visits, photograph children, animals, landscapes and so on.

A successful high street studio photographer could produce at least 3,000 or 4,000 photographic portraits a year, the most prolific operators turning out considerably more. To some extent studio work was seasonal as, until the introduction of electric lighting (typically during the 1890s in many provincial towns), good natural daylight was important and winter days meant shorter business hours, although some commercial photographers worked partly on location, for example photographing weddings or school groups. With studio portraits, often photographers wrote the negative number in pencil or ink on the back of their card mounts and kept the original glass plate negatives, so that customers could order copies later on, by quoting their negative number. The negative numbers written on surviving photographs taken by photographer ancestors whose operative dates have been determined can suggest roughly at what point in their career each photograph was taken.

Most of our photographer ancestors ran modest high street studios in their city or town of residence, serving a regular local clientele, but a minority would have been well-known in their day, particularly if they operated superior establishments and photographed royalty, 'celebrities' and the social elite.

If their work is deemed of special historical and cultural significance their original studio ledgers, account books, photographic negatives and perhaps other records may well have been preserved in a public museum or archive.

Only a very few photographic studios originating in the 19th century are still operational today: one example is Edward Reeves of Lewes in East Sussex, established in 1855, whose present proprietor is the great grandson of the founder and who has preserved the studio's archives. However, sadly most Victorian and Edwardian high street studios have long since gone, their premises demolished or altered beyond recognition, their glass negatives perhaps recycled during World War One and any business papers destroyed. This is frustrating for descendants visiting the location of an ancestor's studio, although if the building still stands traces of the original painted sign may remain on the wall.

**JAYNE SHRIMPTON** is a professional dress historian and picture (photographs and artworks) specialist, a freelance consultant, writer and lecturer working in the family history arena. www.jayneshrimpton.co.uk

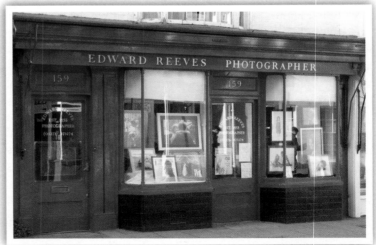

**Edward Reeves' studio in Lewes, East Sussex, founded in 1855, is one of the very few Victorian photography studios still operational in the 21st century**

# Round up the black sheep

*A selection of criminal register records available online may help shed light on a family relative who broke the law and paid the consequences...*

Taken from Home Office Records series and The National Archives *TNA), a data set available online at **www.thegenealogist.co.uk** features more than 89,000 criminal records covering indictable offences in England and Wales between 1782 and 1892. The records also uniquely cover prisoners 'pardoned' and those classed as 'criminal lunatics'. With records dating back to before civil registration began, they are another useful source of early information for family historians.

These records include the following TNA series:

- HO27 – Criminal Registers, England and Wales: registers of all persons in England and Wales charged with indictable offences between 1805 and 1892 showing the results of the trials, the sentences in case of conviction, and dates of execution of persons sentence to death.
- HO13 – Criminal Entry Books: lists of pardons.
- HO20/13 – Prisons Correspondence and Papers: including Bethlehem Hospital ('Bedlam') criminal lunatics and others.
- CRIM1 – Central Criminal Court Depositions: statements on oath used in evidence in trials at the Old Bailey and pardons if granted. Records in this collection do not imply guilt.

There was a recognition that certain crimes were committed by people gripped by insanity and other mental health issues, although crudely described as 'criminal lunatics' at the time.

As an example, the site holds a record for Granville Medhurst, in August 1800. A respected member of society, it appears that Granville had business issues and suffered a breakdown, believing his wife was trying to poison him. He carried an assortment of weapons to their bedroom and then murdered his wife before locking himself in his house.

He was subsequently overpowered and tried for his crime and was described as "elegantly dressed but looking ill and wild" at his trial. His troubled mind and odd behaviour was taken into account at his trial.

The 1800s in England and Wales was a place where it was not difficult to get into trouble and end up facing a severe punishment, perhaps even the death penalty. The infamous system in England and Wales, which relied on its strong deterrent qualities, was dubbed the 'Bloody Code' for good reason.

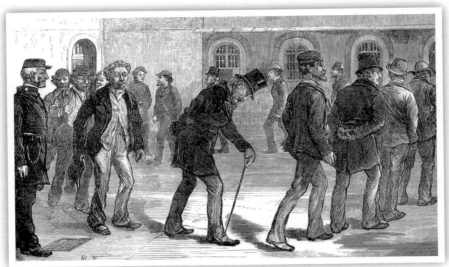

**Prisoners exercising at Newgate Prison, shown in the *Illustrated London News* – available at TheGenealogist**

Despite there being no police force until 1829, there were more than 200 offences which carried the death penalty in 1815 under the 'Bloody Code'. As well as the expected serious crimes such as murder, you could receive the death penalty for stealing, impersonating a Chelsea Pensioner, being in the company of gypsies for a month, stealing livestock, being a pickpocket and also being seen out at night with a 'blackened face' as it was assumed you were a burglar.

As was the tradition in those days, a huge crowd gathered to watch the public executions, regularly in their thousands. Executions were public spectacles, at certain events the wealthy would hire balconies or other vantage points so as to get the best view.

In the case of William and James Lightfoot – see the case study box – a large crowd gathered to watch their final moments. From reports at the time: "Upwards of ten thousand persons had assembled to witness the dreadful end of the unhappy wretches, and but little commiseration was exhibited for their fate."

The new records at TheGenealogist include full information on each case, including names, aliases, the name of the court, the offence committed and the length of the sentence or whether the prisoner was acquitted. There were a variety of sentences for criminal activity ranging from the death penalty to transportation to the colonies to a standard prison sentence.

Statistics show that Wiltshire, Hereford and Essex carried out the greatest number of executions in the 1800s whilst the courts in Lancashire, Yorkshire and Durham spared the lives of the most prisoners.

Not all prisoners were executed, of course, and there were other punishments available including imprisonment or transportation to penal colonies in places such as Australia. Records show, for example, the transportation of one man for seven years for stealing onions and another transported to New South Wales for a term of seven years for stealing table linen.

James Hicks, born in 1804 is another example. He was convicted of stealing two lambs worth 40 shillings at Hertford Assizes, along with three other men. In 1829 this was considered a capital crime and he was initially sentenced to death. But six days later this was commuted to life transportation and he found himself on board a ship, the Mermaid, with nearly 200 other men. TheGenealogist has a copy of this record, as well as his transportation record.

The ship left Sheerness on 2 December 1829, arriving at Port Jackson five months later on 6 May, 1830, with two men having died en route.

TheGenealogist already has a large collection of transportation records

# HIGH-PROFILE MURDERS

Listed in the records at TheGenealogist can be seen a summary of two high profile murder cases at the time. In 1840, brothers William and James Lightfoot robbed and then murdered highly respected timber and general merchant, Nevill Norway (great grandfather of well - known novelist and engineer, Nevill Shute) near Bodmin, Cornwall. They were subsequently tried at Bodmin Court by Mr Justice Coltman on the 30th March, 1840.

With overwhelming evidence against them, the two prisoners faced an inevitable fate. The court notes at the time declared: "The learned judge having then summed up the evidence, the jury returned a verdict of 'Guilty.' Mr Justice Coltman passed the awful sentence of death in the most feeling terms."

Here we see a copy of the record of William Lightfoot at TheGenealogist, with his crime and punishment listed.

Another high profile criminal case listed on TheGenealogist involved William Griffith, who was the first man to be hanged at the new Beaumaris Prison in 1830, for the attempted murder of his wife, Mary. Separated from his wife, he had visited her where she lived with their daughter and had then become extremely violent. The dreadful nature of the attack ensured he was given the death penalty and a big crowd gathered at his execution too.

| Criminal » Criminal Registers & Pardons » Full | |
| --- | --- |
| Forename | William |
| Surname | Lightfoot |
| When Tried | County Assizes 26th Mar |
| Crime | Murder |
| Sentence | Death - Executed 13th Apr 1840 |
| TNA Reference | HO 27 / 60 |
| Year | 1840 |
| County | Cwl |
| Age | 36 |
| Education | Imperfect |

from TNA series HO 10 and HO 11 – in total the site now has around half a million crime-related records.

Not all prisoners were convicted, however. Around 35% of those recorded were actually found 'not guilty', a much higher rate of acquittals than levels today.

The Criminal Records collection at TheGenealogist – under the Court and Criminal Records section – can allow you to discover that missing ancestor and why they may not have appeared on the usual records available to family historians.

With many of our ancestors struggling for survival and living in poverty it is no surprise many fell foul of the law. However, the 'Bloody Code' deterrent that the Victorian authorities so believed in nowadays appears exceptionally harsh and many of our ancestors were transported to the colonies or even worse received the death sentence for the most minor crimes.

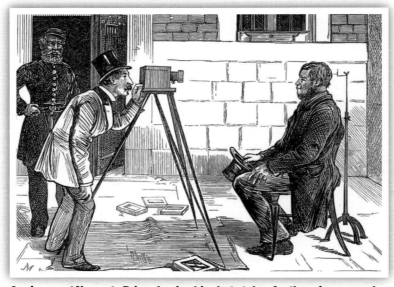

**A prisoner at Newgate Prison having his photo taken for the prison records, from 'sketches of Newgate' published in the Illustrated London News in 1873**

# Forced from home

*Scotland will never forget the brutal evictions of its crofters from the Highlands and islands. Chris Paton explores their legacy and how to trace Scots ancestors who migrated within the country or abroad*

The brutality of the Highland Clearances forms some of the most painful historical memories both within Scotland today and much of the modern Scottish diaspora. Known in Gaelic as 'Fuadach nan Gàidheal' ('The Expulsion of the Gael'), the Clearances were the mass forcible evictions of Highland tenants from their ancient clan lands by those in whom they had previously placed their trust. The reason was the lucrative profitability of sheep farming, achieved through an exercise in ethnic cleansing.

Following the Jacobite campaigns of the early 18th century, the Highland clan system was heavily persecuted, with many of the Gaelic speaking Highlanders having supported the attempts to restore the Stuarts to the throne. As the clan system was ripped apart in the aftermath, the chiefs began to view themselves ever more as landlords, and to rely more on the rents payable by their tenants. Inspired by successful agricultural developments in the Lowlands, many chiefs soon began to conspire to 'improve' their own

'The Emigrants' in Helmsdale, Scotland. An inscription below the statue reads: "'The Emigrants' commemorates the people of the Highlands and Islands of Scotland who, in the face of great adversity, sought freedom, hope and justice beyond these shores..." There is a matching statue in Winnipeg, Canada

Dave Conner

lands to generate more profit, at the expense of their former clansmen. One of the first major clearances happened in Glengarry in 1785, when 500 tenants were evicted to the Canadian province of Ontario (see case study). As the changes were implemented across the Highlands, the tacksmen of the old feudal clan system, who had acted as middle men between their chiefs and the inhabitants, soon found their positions becoming obsolete. Many emigrated and encouraged their own former tenants to follow, forming settlements to which many of those who were later cleared would soon join.

Soon landlords across the Highlands, particularly in Sutherland, were aggressively clearing their lands of tenants to make way for sheep, and with state support. Between 1811 and 1820, homes were torched on the Duke of Sutherland's estates, and at one stage, some 2000 people a day were being cleared from their homes – many were employed on new coastal fishing village developments, and some fled to the main cities to seek work, such as Glasgow and Dundee, but many had no choice but to emigrate. In Easter Ross in 1845, 88 people evicted from Glencalvie sought shelter in Croick churchyard. Graffiti scratched into the church window states "Glencalvie the wicked generation", their plight believed to be a judgement from God. It was not until 1886 that the first security of tenure was finally granted to the few remaining tenants and crofters, following the Crofters Holdings (Scotland) Act.

There is a growing wealth of information available to those wishing to pursue their evicted ancestors' stories. The Am Baile website (**www.ambaile.org**) has many digitised Clearances-related holdings from Highland libraries, as well as a newspaper catalogue listing many contemporary titles, while the British Newspaper Archive contains many accounts of the evictions – several Scottish titles from this can also be freely accessed via the British Library 19th Century Newspaper Collection, accessible through many subscribing local libraries. The Scotsman newspaper is also digitised and available online from 1817 onwards at **http://archive.scotsman.com**. To understand the dramatic changes in many Highland parishes caused by the Clearances, you can consult the free to access Statistical Accounts of Scotland at **http://edina.ac.uk/stat-acc-scot/**), which carry contemporary descriptions of individual parishes, as reported by Church of Scotland ministers in the 1790s and again in the mid-1830s to mid-1840s.

A useful online resource is the Clearances website at **www.theclearances.org** with thousands of stories that can be searched by parish name, a person's name, or by topics such as vessels' names. The site includes detailed descriptions of abandoned Highland settlements, and

# THE STRATHGLASS CLEARANCES

At the start of the 19th century thousands of tenants in Strathglass, near Loch Ness, were evicted from the lands held under William Chisholm, the 24th chief of clan Chisholm. An ill man, much of the daily running of the estate had fallen to his wife, Elizabeth, the daughter of Marjory Macdonnell of Glengarry (known in Gaelic as 'Marsali Bhinneach'). From 1785-1788, Marjory had herself previously cleared five hundred tenants from her own husband's lands at Glen Quoich and forced them to set sail for Canada, after she sold the glen to a sheep farmer from the Lowlands. Glengarry County in Ontario marks the region today where they settled.

Under Marjory's daughter Elizabeth, history repeated itself. In 1801, some eight hundred tenants were forced to sail from Strathglass and surrounding districts for Pictou in Nova Scotia, whilst a year later a further four hundred and seventy three set sail for Ontario and one hundred and twenty eight for Pictou. Five hundred more set sail from Knoydart, whilst in 1803 four more ships with a further five hundred Highlanders from Strathglass set sail for Pictou. It is estimated that in the first decade of the 19th century, some 10,000 inhabitants of Strathglass alone were evicted.

detailed passenger lists from the emigrant vessels, with many articles on what became of those forced overseas. For estate records, the National Records of Scotland (**www.nrscotland.gov.uk**) has an online catalogue listing its holdings, while holdings of local archives can be accessed via the Scottish Archive Network (**www.scan.org.uk**). For the Sutherland estates, where some of the worst atrocities occurred, many papers are available at **http://tinyurl.com/lcopa93**. The Timespan Museum (**http://timespan.org.uk**) at Helmsdale is also worth visiting.

Many of those who were evicted found new lives in Canada, and the main national archive in the country, Library and Archives Canada, has a website at **www.collectionscanada.gc.ca**, which hosts many records such as censuses and early land petitions. The Ontario Genealogical Society can equally help with research enquiries (at **www.ogs.on.ca**), and has many provincial branches, while FamilySearch has many vital records freely accessible at **https://familysearch.org**. If your Highland ancestors migrated to Australia, the National Archives of Australia (**www.naa.gov.au**) site hosts various resources, while the National Library of Australia hosts a guide at **www.nla.gov.au/family-history/genealogy-selected-websites** for all Australian state libraries and archives, as well as various useful databases. The library's impressive Trove facility (**http://trove.nla.gov.au**) is also worth searching, particularly for free newspaper content from 1803 onwards. The vital records for those who were evicted but remained in Scotland are accessible at **www.scotlandspeople.gov.uk**.

**CHRIS PATON** runs the Scotland's Greatest Story family history research service (www.scotlandsgreateststory.co.uk) and is the author of numerous books. He also blogs regularly at http://britishgenes.blogspot.co.uk

# Brought to court

*Nell Darby explores the historic court system,
starting with the Quarter Sessions*

From the 13th century right up until 1971, the court system in England and Wales consisted of three main types – Petty Sessions, where minor offences were heard, Quarter Sessions and Assizes, with the same system existing in Scotland until 1975. Quarter Sessions were the second tier of the system – local county and borough courts, held four times a year. Generally, they were held in each county seat, such as in Oxford or Gloucester.

Each session was, fundamentally, a meeting involving two or more magistrates – Justices of the Peace – where criminal cases would be heard. Each Quarter Session was named after a traditional time of the year when they were held – Epiphany (January to March), Easter (April to June), Midsummer (July to September) and Michaelmas (October to December). At each meeting, there would be at least two magistrates with a chairman, sitting with a jury. These magistrates would also have a clerk, known as the Clerk of the Peace. However, the system was slightly

different in county boroughs, which were allowed their own Quarter Sessions, but with one Recorder instead of a bench of justices.

Quarter Sessions had an important judicial role, not only determining criminal cases, but also referring the most serious crimes, including capital offences (those punishable by the death

**Blind 18th century magistrate Sir John Fielding was chairman of the Quarter Sessions for the City of Westminster. In 1749 he also formed London's first professional police force, the Bow Street Runners, with his brother, the novelist Henry Fielding**

## RESEARCH GUIDE

Most Quarter Sessions records can be found in the relevant county archives. Records from the 18th century can be incomplete, but Victorian-era records are better represented, and more detailed. Recently, some Quarter Session records have been digitised – see www.qurl.com/qsess for some links – as well as The National Archives' criminal registers from 1791 to 1892, which include many Quarter Session records. One such record refers to George Greenwood and Edwin Dean, who were convicted of theft at the West Riding of Yorkshire Epiphany Quarter Sessions in 1831 and sentenced to a month in prison and a whipping each. Surrey History Centre has launched a project to put some of its Quarter Sessions and Assize records from 1848 to 1902 online – if you would like more information, or to get involved with the project, see www.surreycc.gov.uk/recreation-heritage-and-culture/archives-and-history/surrey-history-centre/surrey-records-online.

sentence), to the Courts of Assize. In addition to this role, they also had an important part to play in local administration. The Courts of Quarter Session dealt with taxes, the appointment of local officers and licensing issues, hearing reports from various committees, such as asylum and police committees, setting the county rates, and hearing applications from local town councils regarding the fees charged for hiring local buildings to serve as the locations for Petty Session hearings. In 1860, a committee was appointed at the Oxfordshire Quarter Sessions to report on how best to house the permanent staff of the county militia, illustrating the varied issues that the Quarter Sessions had to deal with.

Quarter Sessions also acted as courts of appeal over decisions made in summary proceedings, or Petty Sessions.

Prior to the 1834 New Poor Law being passed, this often involved issues of poverty, such as when an individual had disagreed with a parish refusing to grant them poor relief. A magistrate at summary proceedings might state that they should be given relief – and a parish that disagreed with that decision might then take the issue forward to Quarter Sessions. Not all appeals involved the Poor Law, though. In 1801, a group of tailors was brought before two London magistrates, accused of "being unlawfully combined to procure an increase of wages, and having refused to work till this increase was obtained" – the 1799 Combination Act having banned collective bargaining. They were convicted and sentenced to two months in the Tothill Fields Bridewell, but allowed "the liberty of appealing" to the Middlesex Quarter Sessions, which were imminent (The Ipswich Journal, 17 January 1801). Unlike other counties, the Middlesex sessions were held eight times a year.

Magistrates also visited prisons to investigate their state and the

# IN THE DORSET DOCK

The Dorset Calendars of Prisoners (available at Dorset History Centre) contain a wealth of detail – such as the case of the Romany gypsy Jimbo Cooper, a 21-year-old illiterate hawker, who was convicted of common assault in 1870. He had beaten and wounded Charles Cobb at Winterborne Kingston and was sentenced to a month's hard labour. The records show that he was also known as Jimbo Light, and that he was of sallow complexion, already balding despite his young age, and just under five feet five inches in height. Earlier in 1870, he had been charged with vagrancy, and served three months in prison. Gypsies were viewed with suspicion in Victorian England, and were often charged with vagrancy as a result of their itinerant lifestyles. The attitudes displayed towards them could both flame aggression and lead to conflict – perhaps such as that displayed between Cooper and Charles Cobb – and also result in a willingness of the courts to both convict and hand down a custodial sentence.

condition of prisoners, reporting back their views to the other magistrates at Quarter Sessions.

The allowances given to prisoners on their discharge from gaol was also an issue discussed at Quarter Sessions.

In 1861, in Oxfordshire, each prisoner was allowed one shilling and a piece of bread on being discharged, but magistrates on one visit noted that this did not take into account that some prisoners lived further away from the prison than others, and might need more money in order to return to their own parish.

All this bureaucracy and administration might make the work of the Quarter Sessions sound quite dry, but newspapers took an increasing amount of interest in their affairs as the 19th century progressed. The press did not just cover Assize trials – they also looked at Quarter Session cases, and the provincial press took great interest in how local administration was dealt with at the Sessions.

However, much of the Victorian media's interest lay in the criminal trials at Quarter Sessions - theft, fraud, and assaults were common offences, but others included sexual assault – such as George Franklyn, 26, who was convicted of raping a young girl at the Surrey County Sessions in 1848 and given six months in prison – and libel or sedition, eg Francis Harker being acquitted of uttering seditious words at the Lancashire Quarter Sessions in 1801.

The Quarter Sessions were not always run perfectly. Prior to the late 18th century, magistrates had been unpaid, and some were accordingly less committed to their work than others, failing to attend court or interfering in cases that other magistrates were supposed to be involved in.

Some were accused of corruption, particularly in more urban areas, thus tarnishing the reputations of those who dispensed justice in a more civilised way. In the 19th century, some of the Courts of Quarter Session had a reputation for bias against certain prisoners, failing to maintain proper records, and not being consistent in setting sentences. Yet it was a system that worked well enough to exist until a fairly recent time, and as a result of its long history, a wealth of records survive. They hold information about a wide variety of individuals – criminals and jurors, magistrates and local officials, witnesses, prosecutors, poor and rich alike. They not only tell the family historian about their ancestors, but also a lot about the world in which they lived, and the society that told them what they could, and could not, do.

**NELL DARBY** (www.nelldarby.com) is a freelance writer, specialising in social history and the history of crime. She has a PhD in gender and the summary process in the 18th century.

# QUARTER SESSIONS ONLINE

There are only selections of Quarter Sessions records available online so far, but among them **TheGenealogist.co.uk** has 16th and 17th century Quarter Session records for Worcestershire. These offer a fascinating glimpse into earlier criminal courts.

This Calendar of the Quarter Sessions covers the period 1593 to 1643. They can be found in the site's Court & Criminal Records collections.

The introductory pages of this dataset provide useful historical background to the subject. For example, in a section on the various types of indictment made at Quarter Sessions – including larceny, robbery with violence, riot, drunkenness and vagrancy, along with other issues such as unlawful enclosure of land or even not going to church – we learn that larceny accounted for around 18% of cases, and was usually theft of farm produce or clothing and goods from homes.

The actual records are organised by year (and can be searched by name). The picture here, for example, shows a variety of indictments from the year 1614.

21. (1614). Indictment of *John Baker* of *Ombersley* Weaver *Alice* his wife *Alice Powell* Spinster and *Thomas Baker* Labourer all of *Ombersley* for assaulting *Humphrey Day* Gentleman at *Ombersley*. A true Bill.                                    XXI. 7.

22. (1614). Indictment of *John Hill* Gentlemen and *William Staunton* Cooper both of *Upton upon Severn* for killing a sore deer in the King's chase called *Malvern Chase*. A true Bill.
XLIII. 20.

23. (1614). Indictment of *William Jennetts* of *Callowhill* for being well fitted to labour and having no land nor goods nor having any art or mystery by which he could gain a livelihood at *Callow Hill* and at other places in the County he was found begging by the Constable and comporting himself as an incorrigible vagabond and mendicant. A true Bill.                      XLIII. 21.

24. (1614). Indictment of *William Child* Gentleman and *Robert Haynes* Labourer both of *Shrawley* for assaulting *John Giles* of *Great Witley* Yeoman at *Hallowe*. A true Bill.    XLIII. 22.

25. (1614). Indictment of *Thomas Pratt* of *Sulley Hill* in the County of *Warwick* Yeoman and *Job Pratt* of *King's Norton* Yeoman for stealing one wheather sheep of a white colour of the value of 10d. out of a certain field called *Garrets Field* at *King's Norton*. A true Bill.                            XLIII. 23.

26. (1614). Indictment of *John Knowles* of the *Lye* Yeoman and *Thomas* . . . . both of *Old Swinford* for assaulting *William Millward* at the *Lye* between 8 and 10 p.m. A true Bill.
XLIII. 24.

27. (1614). Indictment of *Anthony Toy* Yeoman and *Elizabeth* his wife *Elizabeth Warren* wife of *Thomas Warren* Yeoman and *John Toy* Yeoman all of *Wolverley* for assaulting *William Jukes* at *Wolverley*. A true Bill.                           XLIII. 25.

28. (1614). Indictment of *Thomas Webb* Tailor *Edward Pether* Husbandman and *Philip Baynham* Gardener all of *Clifton*

# Petty crimes?

### *Nell Darby looks at Petty Sessions*

P etty sessions were, until 1971, the lowest level of the criminal justice system in the country. They evolved out of the increased workload of magistrates at Quarter Sessions during the 18th century, which led to extra sessions being held in the magistrates' local area to deal with minor offences and local administration by way of summary jurisdiction – meaning that cases could be determined by two or more magistrates without a jury.

The sessions were held for a particular 'hundred' in England, Wales and Ireland – a hundred being the division of a shire for administrative and judicial purposes, akin to a district today. They dealt with petty crimes as common assaults, drunkenness and vagrancy – as well as issues such as licensing and bastardy. Presided over by two or more unpaid magistrates, or by a single stipendiary (paid) magistrate, they had their own clerk who would keep the records of the court, collect fees from those involved in cases, and deal with the administrative work of the court.

Up until the early 19th century, sessions were fairly informal, often held in local inns, and with a great variety in how clerks and magistrates

# THE WITCH & THE BROOMSTICK

Catherine Jones was a woman described by Berrow's Worcester Journal as "a little old woman...[who] stood before the Bench under circumstances which, it is probable, had she lived in the sixteenth century, would have resulted in her seizure by some of the witch-finders, who at that time drove a thriving trade, to the terror of poor old innocent women..." Catherine, who lived in the area of St John's, just west of the city of Worcester, was accused of using her broomstick not for witchcraft but for hitting her neighbour with it after he accused her of sweeping rubbish against his door. This method of assault, together with her age and appearance, led to great interest in the case and the mocking tone of the local press coverage. She was described as having a face "not exactly fashioned according to Hogarth's 'line of beauty', and old and wrinkled withal", the paper using its description to back up its assertion that she would have been identified as a witch in the uncivilised past! Despite her denials and insistence that he brought the first blow against her, and her age and infirmity, she was found guilty and given "her choice – 14 shillings [fine], including expenses, or four days' imprisonment: she preferred the latter, as the least expensive mode of atonement". (Berrow's Worcester Journal, 20 Jan 1842) Catherine's case shows how a trawl of local press coverage can shed light on ancestors who were involved at Petty Sessions; although the press inevitably focused on unusual cases, or unusual defendants – in terms of their appearance, their background, or the charges against them – as the nineteenth century went on, newspapers covered petty sessions more comprehensively, recognising them as a valuable source of information about the local community.

recorded their business. However, the early to mid 19th century saw a raft of legislation passed to make these sessions more uniform and organised. Peel's Larceny Acts in 1827 had the purpose of simplify the criminal law by consolidating earlier acts. There were two acts – one for England, one for Ireland – that gave magistrates at Petty Sessions the right to try some minor offences. The 1848 Summary Jurisdiction Act, often known as Jervis's Act after the then Attorney General, Sir John Jervis, enabled magistrates to issue summons and warrants for indictable offences both if an offence had been committed within their area, or if the suspect in a crime had entered the area. The 1855 Criminal Justice Act then gave magistrates the power to deal with thefts under the value of ten shillings – previously, they had only been able to look at thefts under the value of twelvepence. Historian John Hostettler has described this act as having "paved the way for a huge expansion of the public judicial work of justices during the 19th and 20th centuries".

Victorian press reports shed light on the variety of issues that were dealt with at Petty Sessions. In 1841, in Bristol, one session dealt simply with several cases of turnip and potato thefts. However, the same year, the Eton Petty Sessions dealt with a more serious case of assault – an accusation of cruelty against the master of the Eton Union workhouse towards one of its inmates. The master, Joseph Howe, was accused of having dragged pauper Eliza Wise out of the workhouse nursery, where she had been visiting her child, and locking her in a small, unheated cell. Howe argued, in his defence, that he "was doing no more than my duty" and that Eliza had tried to kick and bite him. But he was found guilty, fined £10, and told that if he did not pay the fine, he would be sent to Aylesbury House of Correction for three months. (London Standard, 4 January 1841)

This case shows how men of all backgrounds could find themselves appearing before the magistrates at petty sessions. At the Cambridge county petty sessions in 1846, a senior fellow of King's College Cambridge, Reverend Lionel Buller, was charged with trespassing on various people's lands in search of game, despite not being qualified to game. He was convicted, and fined five shillings for each of the three charges, plus costs, and 40 shillings plus costs for the fourth charge. These fines were levied despite the magistrates knowing that Buller was "destitute of funds from his property being locked up by a Chancery suit" in court, and that his inability to pay fines would result in his being sent to prison. However, the magistrates' hands in such cases were tied. The fines for gaming offences were clearly set out in law, and in addition, landowners often pressurised the magistrates – men from their own backgrounds – to apply the law strictly. (The Preston Guardian, 10 Oct 1846)

Petty Sessions continued until 1974, when they were replaced by magistrates' courts – three years after the 1971 Courts Act abolished Assizes and Quarter Sessions, replacing these with crown courts. However, magistrate courts still continue to deal with the least serious offences, that can be heard without a jury, and magistrates can still only issue certain punishments, just like their predecessor, the Petty Sessions.

# WHERE TO FIND THE RECORDS

Primarily, Petty Sessions records are kept by local county record offices and few have been put online. Oxfordshire holds records from 1828 up to the 1970s, including minute books and registers. The latter tend to have more information about the parties involved and the offence. Formal records of proceedings often survive from no earlier than the mid-nineteenth century, and it was only after 1879 that standard methods of record keeping at petty sessions were adopted. The survival of records within a specific county really does vary – some of the Glamorgan petty sessions minute books only survive from the early 20th century, whereas those for the Newcastle and Ogmore Petty Sessions survive from 1836 onwards. Some Irish Petty Sessions records can be found online. These include two courts - in Meath and Tipperary - that have pre-famine records. For links to the limited Petty Sessions available online, see www.genguide.co.uk/source/petty-sessions-crime-criminals-amp-courts/148/

# The flying judges

*Nell Darby concludes her series on the historic tiers of the court system with a look at the Assizes, which saw presiding judges travelling around the country*

U ntil 1971, the Courts of Assize – or Assizes – were held around England and Wales to try the most serious offences, such as homicide, infanticide, highway robbery, rape and grand larceny (the theft of items over the value of 12d, a crime that was once a capital offence). They also dealt with civil disputes over land or money.

The Assizes were presided over by visiting judges – the Justices of Assize – appointed by the King's Bench to travel on 'circuits' through groups of counties. Each county would have an assize, most commonly in the main county town. There were six circuits – the Home, Norfolk and South-Eastern; Midland; Northern and North-Eastern; Oxford; Welsh including Chester; and the Western Circuit. The Home area covered Essex, Hertfordshire, Kent, Surrey and Sussex; the Western circuit covered Cornwall, Devon, Dorset, Somerset, Hampshire and Wiltshire, together with the cities and towns of Bristol, Exeter, Poole and

**The Justices of Assize in procession at Lincoln Cathedral on 'Assize Sunday' in 1845, from the *Illustrated London News***

# THE DRUNKEN WIFE-BEATER

At the Durham Assizes in November 1900, 28 cases were heard, but only one was of murder. John Bowes, a 50-year-old bricklayer, was indicted for the wilful murder of his wife Isabella, 43, at Dawdon on 8 September 1900. John appeared on 24 November for what was described by the local press as "a shocking crime". John was described as a lazy, jealous and bad-tempered man, whereas his wife had been "a respectable, hardworking woman" who kept the family afloat. Dawdon was a mining community, and part of the beach was a dumping ground for waste coal. Isabella had earned five shillings a day by finding bits of coal on the beach and selling it on. The couple had been married for 26 years, but Isabella had long been unhappy. On 21 August 1900, after a series of arguments and threats from John, she left him. Three weeks later, Isabella was, as usual, on the beach picking coal, when John – seen by a witness – joined her, striking her several times with a piece of wood so heavy that he had to hold it in both hands. Isabella died later in the local infirmary, having never having gained consciousness. The couple's 20-year-old daughter, Annie, was called to give evidence at the trial, where she described years of enduring her father's drunkenness and physical abuse. Neighbours described hearing John's threats towards his wife, and their previous arguments. The jury found John Bowes guilty of wilful murder and the judge passed the sentence of death, saying he was sorry to say that the case "was only another of the many cases he had had to deal with in this and other counties, whenever people were brought to the scaffold from undue use of drink". (North-Eastern Daily Gazette, 24 November 1900) James Bowes was hanged on 12 December 1900 at Durham.

Southampton. Pairs of judges would work their way round the circuits to try prisoners and hear and determine cases. Assizes were usually held twice a year, with each circuit could last between a fortnight and a month, depending on how many cases there were to be heard.

Some areas of the country were not part of the assize system: Lancashire, Durham and Cheshire were separate originally; the Palatinate of Chester came under the system in 1830; but Durham and Lancaster didn't until the 1870s. London was also slightly different: it was not historically part of the Assize system until 1834, when the Central Criminal Court – formerly the Old Bailey – became the equivalent of an assize court not just for London but also for part of the surrounding counties of Essex, Kent and Surrey.

Prisoners brought to trial at the Assizes had already been through a long-established criminal justice process. Although some men might be indicted for a crime on a coroner's inquisition – at an inquest – many others, on being suspected of a crime, would be brought before magistrates where they would be examined.

For example, in January 1851, six men were charged with murdering a gamekeeper at Elveden in Suffolk. They were initially brought before four magistrates at the Station House in nearby Mildenhall.Depositions – witness statements – had already been taken, and were read by the magistrates. Others were called, including a surgeon, police officer, and the wife of one of the accused, as well as some of the men's neighbours. The prisoners were allowed to question the witnesses before the magistrates deliberated. They then announced that three men would be discharged, but the other three committed for trial at the next Assizes. (Bury and Norwich Post and Suffolk Herald, 8 January 1851)

The process had its problems, and labouring, uneducated men could be at a disadvantage. One of the men committed for the murder above was asked to question witnesses, but was seen to hesitate: he "did not appear to understand how he was to act. He said he had never been up for anything before, and he did not know what to ask". There are also problems for genealogists looking at assize records, such as indictments, for personal information; as historian JS Cockburn established, many indictments have been found where the defendant's occupation or abode is "entirely fallacious" – perhaps because officials were filling in details quickly to meet the minimal requirements of the system. The National Archives also warns that the use of aliases or false details can make the material unreliable. But where details can be corroborated, the records of this now extinct court can make distant ancestors come back to life.

## ASSIZES ONLINE

In 1834, the Central Criminal Court, based in the Sessions House at the Old Bailey, became, in effect, the assize court for London as well as parts of surrounding counties. The Old Bailey Online website (www.oldbaileyonline.org) is a free, fully searchable resource that has the trial reports of thousands of cases heard here. Although it is best known for its earlier records – 17th and 18th century Old Bailey cases – it actually covers cases up to 1913. Records of the Guildhall sessions, which covered the City of London, are held at London Metropolitan Archives. The Capital Punishment UK website (www.capitalpunishmentuk.org) also has details of some assize cases, and a good introduction to the assize circuit. For more online resources, see www.genguide.co.uk/source/assize-records-crime-criminals-amp-courts/76/

# Trade secrets

*Apprenticeships have been a key part of many of our forebears'
lives. Many apprenticeship records are available online*

Apprenticeships have a long history, and had become very popular by the 14th century. To become an apprentice, the parents or guardians of the minor would speak with a guild's master craftsman to agree the conditions and price, which would then be recorded in an indenture. The apprentice would usually learn for 5-9 years, depending on the trade and the agreed contract. The typical apprenticeship lasted from age 14 to 21.

Records of apprenticeships in some cases date back to the 13th century when the trade guild system began, although many apprenticeships – such as those between fathers and sons – were inevitably never recorded.

From 1563, when the Statute of Artificers and Apprentices was passed, it actually became illegal to enter a trade without undertaking an apprenticeship (although there were some exceptions).

From 1601, 'parish' apprenticeships under Elizabethan poor law came

to be used as a way of providing for poor, illegitimate and orphaned children of both sexes alongside the regular system of skilled apprenticeships, which tended to provide for boys from slightly more affluent backgrounds. These parish apprenticeships, which could be created with the assent of two Justices of the Peace, supplied apprentices for occupations of lower status such as farm labouring, brickmaking and menial household service. Some records of these survive in local record offices.

The most useful set of apprenticeship records available to family historians, however, comes in the form of Stamp Duty records kept from 1710 to 1811.

These were registers kept by the Board of Stamps of the monies received in payment of the duty on apprentices' indentures under the Statute of Anne and subsequent acts.

In addition to the sums received, the registers record the names, addresses and trades of the masters, the names of the apprentices and the dates of the articles. Until the year 1752, the names of the apprentices' parents are typically given, but after that year very rarely.

These records are held by The National Archives at Kew in series IR1. The volumes consist of City or Town Registers, October 1711 to January 1811, with daily entries of the indentures upon which duty was paid in London; Country Registers, May 1710 to September 1808 with entries, made in London, of the indentures upon which duty had been paid to district collectors and which were afterwards sent up by them in batches to be stamped; and a Ledger of Duties Paid on Indentures, 1799 to 1802.

Where the Stamp Duty was paid in London, entries are in the city (town) registers. Where it was paid elsewhere, entries are in the country registers. If the apprenticeship was in Middlesex or one of the home counties the duty may have been paid in London and the details entered in one of the London registers.

The apprentice training route has for many people set them on their way in their working life or as a way of developing others. From James Hargreaves (inventor of the spinning jenny) to Thomas Yeoman (first President of The Society of Civil Engineers), to Sir Michael Caine (who started as an apprentice plumber) and Beatle George Harrison who was an apprentice electrician, they have all experienced the apprenticeship programme. Many apprentices did their training, worked their way up and then took on apprentices themselves.

This traditional way of training young people is now regaining popularity as the benefits our ancestors recognised are re-introduced as a way of giving people a start in a career.

Leading data website **TheGenealogist.co.uk** has a collection of more one million apprentice and master records from the Stamp Duty registers. The site has also applied its advanced keyword search technology to census records of apprentices. These sources combined make more than two million searchable records – the largest searchable collection of apprentice records available online, covering the two centuries from 1710 to 1911.

The records are available at **www.thegenealogist.co.uk** to Diamond subscribers in the site's Master Search and under the 'Occupation Records' section. You can search for both apprentices and masters.

TheGenealogist allows you to view the full transcript of an apprentice-ship record to see more details of your ancestors apprenticeship – including when they started their training, the 'Master' who trained them and how long their apprenticeship was scheduled to be.

From 1710-1811 the master paid Stamp Duty for taking on the apprentice. The payment could be made at the start of the apprenticeship or any time up to one year after the expiry of the indenture. You might therefore need to search the records of several years' payments to find a particular entry.

The rate was 6d (sixpence) for every £1 under £50 which the master received for taking on the apprentice, and the rate of 1s (one shilling) for every £1 above £50. The indentures on which duty was payable cover Great Britain but not Ireland.

You may not be able to find records for common trades such as weaving or other 18th century industries because:
• Informal indentures became increasingly common with fathers often teaching sons and nephews
• The Statute of Apprentices only applied to trades which existed when it was passed in 1563
• Masters did not have to pay Stamp Duty on the indentures of apprentices taken on at the common or public charge of any township or parish or by or out of any public charity. (In such cases, local or charity records, if they survive, are likely to be the only source of information.)

The available apprenticeship records are nonetheless an invaluable tool for family historians, offering new avenues for research and helping you break down brick walls.

# The family killer

*Paul Matthews explores how typhus ravaged many of our ancestors' lives through a sad example from his own research*

This is the story of an English soldier and his Scottish wife who both died from typhus within the same year – and the wider threat this deadly disease posed in past centuries.

Stephen Kilminster (c1822-76) came from Wootton Bassett, Wiltshire, where the 1841 census shows him living with his family. In 1842 he joined the 51st Regiment of Foot at Chippenham, and served two years in Australia. He deserted in May 1843, re-joining in August. He was court martialled and imprisoned, but spent 13 years in the East Indies, where we find him in 1861, with the 74th Foot (Highlands) in India.

He was next in Burma and was "in possession of a medal and clasp for the capture of Pegu", for which it was said "he still claims prize money". Stephen fought in the Second Burmese War (1852-53), which ended in the annexation of Pegu province. Pegu town was taken on 3 June after fierce fighting near the Shwemdawdaw Pagoda.

In 1864 private 3613 left the army in Aberdeen aged 39. That year he married Helen Mennie (1842-77), a domestic servant aged 22. Aberdonians usually married within their area with little mixing from elsewhere in Scotland, but there was an occasional sprinkling of English

blood. They had four children and the 1865 birth certificate of their son, William, records Stephen as a Chelsea Pensioner: professional soldiers serving full terms were generally awarded 'out pensions' from the Chelsea Hospital.

Stephen was luckily to avoid typhus as a soldier. More soldiers died of typhus in Napoleon's retreat Russian retreat than were killed fighting, and typhus was known as the American Civil War's devastating 'camp fever'. Ironically, after his years of service, Stephen succumbed while living a peaceful life in Aberdeen.

Typhus was common on 1800s death certificates. Its onset was sudden and symptoms included delirium, abdominal pain, fever, nausea and a rash. In pre-antibiotic days it was often fatal. Not to be confused with typhoid, an unrelated disease, it is one of several diseases caused by Rickettsia bacteria. Epidemic typhus is caused by Rickettsia prowazekii and spread by human body lice. These lice were then an unpleasant fact of life especially in conditions of poor hygiene, over-crowding and poverty. Found in the bedding and clothing of infected people, they caused an intense itching accompanied by small bites which developed into a rash.

Typhus appears on death certificates under many names, sometimes referring to the same or a similar disease and sometimes different conditions – and the different terms are used inconsistently.

You may find: spotted ague, abdominal typhus, African tick typhus and scrub typhus (not typhus but related diseases), typhus carcerum or jail fever, war fever, endemic or murine typhus, epidemic typhus also called European or louse born typhus, typhus ichteroides (yellow fever), typhus icterus (indicating jaundice), and typhus recurrens and Brill-

## RESOURCES

- A Brief Memoir Concerning the Typhus Fever Prevalent in Aberdeen during the Years 1818-1819 by George Kerr.
- The Encyclopaedia of Plague and Pestilence by George C Kohn
- A History of Epidemics in Britain, Volume I, by Charles Creighton
- Many military records can be accessed at **www.thegenealogist.co.uk** including Army Lists from the 17th to 20th centuries and many Rolls of Honour; the site also produces surname distribution maps for England and Wales – useful for a rare name such as Kilminster
- The Aberdeen and North East Family History Society has premises in central Aberdeen at 164 King Street, AB24 5BD and includes a well-stocked library; www.anesfhs.org.uk
- A key resource for Scottish family history is The National Records of Scotland at www.nrscotland.gov.uk. On site research can be carried out in Edinburgh search rooms at General Register House and West Register House.

Zinsser disease (recurrent forms).

There was an Irish typhus epidemic in 1816-1819, and another associated with the potato famine in 1846-1849. It spread to England as 'Irish fever', hitting the crowded lower classes worst. Typhus is recorded in Aberdeen in 1818-19 and returned as part of a Scotland-wide epidemic in 1840 when 535 cases were admitted to its two fever wards. There were later outbreaks in 1863-66, in 1846-8 (where it spread to Northern Ireland and was known as 'the Scotch fever'), and in 1882 in the crowded Gallowgate and Causeway End areas.

The 1871 census shows Stephen and Elizabeth living in Commerce Street; they later moved to Queen Street. They had escaped the 1860s typhus outbreak, but from the informative Scottish death certificates we learn that Stephen died aged 54 on 17 September 1876, at the Royal Infirmary, Aberdeen of typhus lasting eight days. Aged just 32, Helen died the following year at the same infirmary, from 'typhus fever' lasting 18 days. The same doctor certified both deaths.

Typhus left the Kilminsters' four children orphaned. In the 1881 census two of the boys were boarding with elderly crofters – sometimes orphans were assigned to an elderly couple – and another aged 16 worked in a comb factory. The daughter, Harriet, aged nine, was resident at the Female Orphan Institute, although by 1891 she lived with her grandmother.

The Aberdeen Kilminsters survived and their numbers grew. The surname is rare but Grampian is one of the five British counties where you are most likely to find it.

**PAUL MATTHEWS** is a freelance writer who has written widely on family history and has had jokes broadcast in BBC radio. He is married and lives in Cheshunt.

# The skill of search

*Here are some tips to get the most out of the unique
Master Search features at TheGenealogist*

K nowing how to use search engines is a skill in itself – although we all expect to simply throw in a name, click a button and get the right results, there are techniques which can help. Many search engines – including Google – offer a wealth of 'hidden' features for refining your results (or widening them). This is very much the case with the incredibly powerful Master Search at leading data website **www.thegenealogist.co.uk**.

In the case of census records before 1911, remember that the enumeration books are only a copy of the individual household census

**The Genealogist's Master Search includes powerful features for finding your family. Here, for example, a search for Elizabeth Kennedy brings up people called Betsy and Isabella, both variants of the name, if we tick the 'Include Nicknames' box. Results can also be widened or refined by the careful use of the wildcard '*', eg 'Kenn*' to catch all people whose surnames begin with those letters (note that this can't be used at the same time as phonetic or nickname searches)**

forms, so the enumerator may have transcribed the information incorrectly in the first place or the information may simply have been wrong. Also some people managed to miss being enumerated at all, whilst others manage to be in two places at once.

To help find those elusive ancestors requires thinking about how can you match all possible miss interpretations of someone's name. Better still is thinking about what is more likely to be recorded accurately. The first option is to maximise the number of possible entries by using various facilities built into Master Search:

**Wildcards:** Try using the wildcard character '*' to match any number of characters after the first 3. Thus 'Ken*' will match Kent, as well as Kendall and Kennedy. This will pull up entries which may have been spelt incorrectly in the original enumerators books.

**Nicknames:** Try ticking this option to search for nicknames which may have been used instead of the standard name – for example Betty, Betsy, Beth or Liz for Elizabeth.

**Phonetic matching:** Try ticking this option to search for different spellings of a name. For example, Bailey and Bayley. This technique uses the sound of a name to find similar matches which produces much more accurate results compared to the name variant matches used by other websites.

**Keywords:** Keywords are a great way to refine your results, especially when searching for a common name such as Smith. Just enter any piece of information that would be found on a record; such as occupation, street or place.

The above search options will help to improve the number of results you get. If you get too many results, try adding in extra search criteria, eg a year range, try unticking variants, or adjust your wildcard search. For example if you have hundreds of results with 'Ken*' and you are looking for possible mis-spellings of 'Kennedy', try 'Kenn*' instead.

These techniques should help you find the person you are looking for.

Don't forget to use the Master Search to check out the adjacent counties, too. Another good alternative strategy is to look for the husband/wife or son/daughter to locate the family. Master Search uniquely allows you to search for either a person or a family, or even to find anyone at a particular address in census records.

# The back-up brigades

*Did you have an ancestor who was a part-time soldier in the late 18th Century? Militia muster records online could help you advance your research*

The tradition of militias in England, providing a reserve force of non-professional soldiers in times of crisis, dates back to Anglo-Saxon times. By the 16th century, the militia had become an important institution in English life. Now the largest collection of militia records available online has been released at **www.thegenealogist.co.uk**, and could help you explore your 18th century ancestors.

The early militia was organized on the basis of the shire county, and was one of the responsibilities of the Lord Lieutenant, a royal official (usually a trusted nobleman). Each of the county hundreds was likewise the responsibility of a Deputy Lieutenant, who relayed orders to the justices of the peace or magistrates. Every parish furnished a quota of eligible men, whose names were recorded on muster rolls. Likewise, each

**Thomas Rowlandson's depiction of a review of the Northampton militia in the late 18th century**

household was assessed for the purpose of finding weapons, armour, horses, or their financial equivalent, according to their status. The militia was supposed to be mustered for training purposes from time to time, but this was rarely done. The militia regiments were consequently ill-prepared for an emergency, and could not be relied upon to serve outside their own counties.

After the English Civil War, Parliament distrusted the creation of a large standing army not under civilian control. Both Whigs and Tories preferred a small standing army under civilian control for defensive deterrence and to prosecute foreign wars, a large navy as the first line of national defence, and a militia composed of their neighbours as additional defence and to preserve domestic order. The English Bill of Rights of 1689 declared "that the raising or keeping a standing army

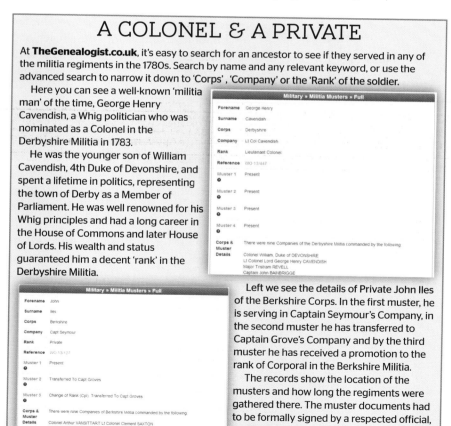

# A COLONEL & A PRIVATE

At **TheGenealogist.co.uk**, it's easy to search for an ancestor to see if they served in any of the militia regiments in the 1780s. Search by name and any relevant keyword, or use the advanced search to narrow it down to 'Corps', 'Company' or the 'Rank' of the soldier.

Here you can see a well-known 'militia man' of the time, George Henry Cavendish, a Whig politician who was nominated as a Colonel in the Derbyshire Militia in 1783.

He was the younger son of William Cavendish, 4th Duke of Devonshire, and spent a lifetime in politics, representing the town of Derby as a Member of Parliament. He was well renowned for his Whig principles and had a long career in the House of Commons and later House of Lords. His wealth and status guaranteed him a decent 'rank' in the Derbyshire Militia.

Left we see the details of Private John Iles of the Berkshire Corps. In the first muster, he is serving in Captain Seymour's Company, in the second muster he has transferred to Captain Grove's Company and by the third muster he has received a promotion to the rank of Corporal in the Berkshire Militia.

The records show the location of the musters and how long the regiments were gathered there. The muster documents had to be formally signed by a respected official, such as a Justice of the Peace.

**A Derbyshire militiaman in 1780**

within the kingdom in time of peace, unless it be with consent of Parliament, is against law...".

The Militia Act of 1757 created a more professional national military reserve. Better records were kept, and the men were selected by ballot to serve for longer periods. Proper uniforms and better weapons were provided, and the force was 'embodied' from time to time for training sessions.

In a time of increasing political uncertainty abroad it was felt necessary to have the security of a 'backup', part-time force in case of invasion. Britain was often in military conflict with the French and Dutch and it was felt that a homeland security force was essential to guard home soil.

The militia were posted at several strategic locations, in particular the South Coast of England, Wales and Ireland. A number of camps were held at Brighton, where the militia regiments were reviewed by royalty – this is the origin of the song 'Brighton Camp'. The militia could not be forced to serve overseas, but it was seen as a vital training reserve for the army. Bounties were offered to men who opted to subsequently 'exchange' from the militia to the regular army.

In the colonies, the British set up the use of militias to protect their interests, as regular troops were often too far away to be used. This was particularly seen in North America in the French and Indian Wars before 1774. The loyal militia were often the primary 'English' force in the field.

Militias based in England were little used but still felt necessary. The only action on home soil was the Battle of Jersey in 1781, when the Royal Militia of the Island of Jersey combined with regular British Army troops to repel a joint French and Dutch invasion force. The British commander, Major Francis Peirson, was killed as the battle reached its climax, but victory was gained and the invading forces defeated. The Battle of Jersey reinforced the perceived need for militia help.

The Militia Act of 1757 offered all 'able-bodied' men to serve in the militia at home in order to counter any threat arising while the majority of the regular army was stationed abroad. Lists of eligible men in each parish were known as 'militia ballot lists' and from these, the men actually chosen appeared in the militia lists, of which more than 58,000 now appear online at TheGenealogist.

The militias were funded by Land Tax and received a 'marching tax' and expenses for attending meetings. As the militias were part-time they were called up at times of war, such as the latter stages of the American War of Independence when France and Spain both declared war on Britain and there was a national threat to the country. In between wars, the militias were disbanded and not required to meet.

The records on TheGenealogist are a list of four significant 'musters' or organised meetings in which all the regiments of the militias are brought together and names are recorded. These records provide us with a snapshot of who was serving, with what regiment, and in some case the dates they were serving, when they were discharged, or if they died in service.

These records cover musters in 1781 and 1782 and form the largest number of surviving records available for this era. They join the largest collection of Army Lists available online, establishing TheGenealogist as a major military research site.

The records cover people from all walks of life who made up the officers and men. From MPs to landowners, from carpenters to labourers, if they were physically up to it, they could be selected for the militia.

Regiments covering all of England and Wales are represented in these new records. The original records are from The National Archives series WO 13 and feature the muster and pay lists of all members of the militias. Men received 'marching money' when the militia was mobilised and were paid expenses for local meetings. County regiments, although recruited locally, often served away from home and these indexes tell precisely where, under whom and on what dates the men were mustered.

These newly online militia lists can further help track the movements and lives of our ancestors before census and civil registration times.

# Grande dame of the seas

*The SS Great Britain took thousands of people to new
lives in America and Australia – here we explore the archives
of her distinguished career*

Isambard Kingdom Brunel's SS Great Britain is one of the most important historic ships in the world. When she was launched in 1843, she was called "the greatest experiment since the creation".

No one had ever designed so vast a ship, nor had the vision to build it of iron. Brunel fitted her with a 1000 hp steam engine, the most powerful yet used at sea. He also gave her a screw propeller, the newest invention in maritime technology.

SS was originally designed for the Great Western Steamship Company's transatlantic service between Bristol and New York. She was the first iron steamer to cross the Atlantic, which she did in 1845, in the time of 14 days, and from 1845 to 1854 was the longest passenger ship in the world.

In 1852, Gibbs, Bright & Co purchased the SS Great Britain to use for carrying emigrants to Australia. On the Australia run the ship was to rely more on sail power than on her steam engine – this would save money. An extra upper deck was built, so that the ship could carry up to 700 passengers.

On her first voyage to Melbourne, she carried 630 emigrants. She excited great interest there, with 4,000 people paying a shilling each to inspect her. She operated on the England-Australia route for almost 30 years, interrupted only by two relatively brief sojourns as a troopship during the Crimean War and the Indian Mutiny.

On one typical voyage, leaving Liverpool on 21 October 1861, she carried

# SS GREAT BRITAIN & BRUNEL ONLINE

The SS Great Britain launched its own weekly newspaper for passengers in 1865, and data website **TheGenealogist.co.uk** has several digitised issues of the newspaper, which are available for all Diamond subscribers. These include interesting details about the ship and its progress, as well as incidents onboard and events such as birth and deaths. The last issue of the journey also provides a passenger list with names of those in intermediate, second cabin and saloon. As with all records at TheGenealogist, the collection can be searched by name.

The newspaper gives a fascinating snapshot of life on board. The editions from the first voyage covered, in 1865, include a history of the ship to date, announcements and reports of entertainments on board, details of the distance travelled each week and news from around the world.

TheGenealogist also has a wealth of resources for exploring the life and times of the SS Great Britain's creator, engineering legend Isambard Kingdom Brunel.

Brunel was born on 9 April 1806 in Portsmouth, to Sir Marc Brunel and his wife Sophia Kingdom. Marc Brunel was a well respected French engineer, who left his home country during the French Revolution to settle in England, and was knighted at Buckingham Palace in March 1841. Marc can be found in the collection 'Knights of England 1127-1904' at TheGenealogist.

One of Isambard's most significant projects while working with his father's company was assisting in the construction of the Thames Tunnel at Rotherhithe, at the age of 20. The Thames Tunnel was the first tunnel to be successfully built below a river, and later became part of the London Underground network. In 1829, Brunel won a competition to design the Clifton Suspension Bridge in Bristol, and joined the Great Western Railway Company in 1833. He was involved in numerous railway projects during his life, engineering over 1,200 miles of railway, including the main line between Bristol and London, which included viaducts, bridges and tunnels.

Brunel (pictured in 1857) was also involved in the re-design and construction of several major docks such as Bristol and Cardiff, and became involved in three major ship-building projects with the Great Western Steamship Company, of which the SS Great Britain was one.

Both Isambard and Sir Marc Brunel are recorded in the Dictionary of National Biography, part of the Biography Records collection at TheGenealogist. Information recorded in these records can include births, baptisms, marriages and burials, education, details of siblings and other family members. Some entries also give details of parents with important dates in their lives and their occupation. Brunel and his wife can also be found in marriage and census records at the site, and his obituary is recorded in an 1859 issue of the Illustrated London News, also available at TheGenealogist.

a crew of 143, 544 passengers (including the first English cricket team to visit Australia), a cow, 36 sheep, 140 pigs, 96 goats and 1,114 chickens, ducks, geese and turkeys. The journey took 64 days.

In 1872 the SS Great Britain's long-standing captain, John Gray, disappeared in mysterious circumstances which have never been fully explained. After 30 years as a passenger ship, SS Great Britain was converted to carry cargo. Between 1882 and 1886 she carried a variety of exports such as coal and wheat between England and the West Coast of America.

Her long working life finally ended in 1933, and she was abandoned to rust. Eventually, an expert salvage team managed to refloat the SS Great Britain on 13 April 1970. She crossed the Atlantic sitting on a huge floating pontoon pulled by tugs. This amazing salvage brought her 8,000 miles home to her birth place in Bristol, where she remains as a museum.

Part of Brunel's vision, when he watched the SS Great Britain launch into Bristol docks in 1843, was to connect people and families from around the world. 170 years on his magnificent ship is still achieving that goal, but with a modern twist. The maritime curators at the Brunel Institute are able to very quickly establish whether somebody travelled on the ship, which voyage they were on and what happened while they were at sea. Already they have been able to help many people, from as far away as Australia, to track down their relatives. People can unveil all sorts of information about their family history with a free visit to the Brunel Institute. This is situated next to the SS Great Britain on Bristol's Great Western Dockyard and is home to an extensive archive of documents and artefacts relating to the ship and her history, including passenger and crew lists which can be used to track ancestors.

With thanks to Dominic Rowe and colleagues at the SS Great Britain Trust and Brunel Institute.

# RESEARCH RESOURCES

The Brunel Institute has a wide variety of records of interest to family historians with crew or passenger connections to the SS Great Britain, including:

- Copies of the passenger lists (the originals are held by the State Library of Victoria, Australia) for most outward journeys of SS Great Britain from Liverpool to Melbourne, dating from 1852 to 1875.
- Voyage boxes – these contain copies of contemporary accounts (passenger diaries and letters, newspaper articles, crew lists, ship log books, photographs, etc.) of individual voyages from 1843 until 1886.
- Original archive documents including passenger letters and diaries, ship's log books, certificates of character and certificates of discharge for crew members, and contemporary newspaper accounts of the construction, launch and voyages of SS Great Britain.
- The University of Bristol Brunel Collection – currently on loan to the Brunel Institute. This mainly concerns Isambard Kingdom Brunel's involvement in the design and construction of ss Great Britain. This collection does have some material relating to her early voyages to New York.

# Know your place

*Researching local history is a key skill for family historians and is a rewarding activity in its own right, as Jill Morris explains*

Broadly speaking, local history focuses on a geographical area. It is usually concerned either with past events in a locale, the people who lived there, or its cultural and social background. However, 'local' shouldn't mean parochial, or limited: regional happenings should be placed within the wider national context. For example, attacks on mills in Huddersfield in 1812 make little sense if not seen as part of that decade's Luddite rebellions against labour-saving machinery!

### A history of local history

Until the later 1800s history was the domain the ivory towers of academia and was a serious discipline exploring world events. Any interest in a specific location would have been dismissed as a pastime, perhaps one suited to those with time on their hands, such as amateur antiquarians. However, 1899 saw the start of the Victoria History of the Counties of England project, which aimed to record a history of England's counties

Look and Learn

**Local history often brings change to light. This 1859 scene shows a ruined stagecoach in a farmyard with a brand new railway station in the background**

# FULNECK MORAVIAN SETTLEMENT

Close to Pudsey in West Yorkshire lies the village of Fulneck, founded by descendants of a protestant Christian denomination whose members fled persecution in Moravia. Moravian missionaries settled in Fulneck in 1744 on land donated by Benjamin Ingham, an Anglican clergyman.

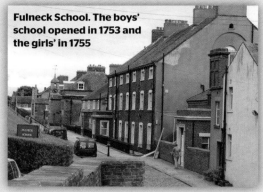

**Fulneck School. The boys' school opened in 1753 and the girls' in 1755**

Hailing from a nearby town, I have been to Fulneck many times. A visit is like stepping back in time; the main thoroughfare has changed little since the 1740s. However, until recently I knew little of the settlement's history and how this devout group wound up overlooking a green valley midway between Leeds and Bradford.

During Heritage Open Day weekend in September 2012 members of the church and local residents organised tours of the settlement, including the school, founded in the 1750s, the Moravian burial ground, chapel and museum.

Living in the locale made visiting and undertaking this initial research – including talking to the knowledgeable guides – straightforward, but how could I find out more? A search of the ARCHON database directed me to the West Yorkshire Archive Service website, www.wyjs.org.uk, and a further keyword search for Fulneck in the online catalogue generated lists of relevant holdings, including lists of pupils at the school, the church's marriage, baptism and burial records, wills, early correspondence and much more. Some records were digitised; others would require a visit to the archives.

Of course, there is much more to uncover, both online and off. This small example not only shows how fascinating local history can be, but the ways in which the shaping of a locality is closely tied to events in the wider world.

in honour of the Queen. The first volume was published in 1901 and the project is still running, so it is well worth consulting the relevant volume when you begin to research – see **www.victoriacountyhistory.ac.uk**. Although these publications elevated local history above the hobbyist's domain, it was 1947 before a British university – Leicester – opened a local history department. Although it's still not widely catered for by higher education, local history is recognised as a fascinating, worthwhile pursuit enjoyed by millions, many of whom are also family historians.

### How to go about it

The mainstays of British local history are local studies libraries, county records offices (CROs) and the many societies or groups that have been set up to encourage and assist those researching an area… and, of course, the internet. More on that later. However, while the amount of digitised material available makes local research possible from anywhere in the world, if you are able to visit the location you are interested in, do. There's no substitute for seeing first-hand the places you're researching.

To help you to get started, find out which library in your domain of study has a local studies section (usually the main branch). If you can, visit and find out what records are available. Alternatively, email, telephone, or consult the relevant website. It's likely that you will find varied collections of books and printed items, newspapers and maps, photos and oral history sources as well as advice on what other

# PLACES & PEOPLE ONLINE

Records of local and family history are often intertwined, and understanding one can often help with the other. Popular data website **TheGenealogist.co.uk**, for example, has a wealth of records which can help you understand the relationships between people and place.

To return to the example of Fulneck, for instance, the Moravian community would be classed as Nonconformists. Many of their records can thus be found in the site's unique collection of Nonconformist and Nonparochial baptism, marriage and burial registers. Right, for example, is a 1770 burial register from Fulneck's Moravian Church (one of the names is Sarah Cennick, daughter of the Moravian convert and evangelist John Cennick. The priest who recorded the register was William Charlesworth, a relative of Brother James Charlesworth who ran a cloth weaving business to support Fulneck's Moravian community financially.

The second image shows how TheGenealogist's powerful Master Search can also be used to further research of this kind. For example, entering 'Fulneck' as a keyword and 'Yorkshire' as the county in a census search brings up an at-a-glance list of the village's population, which one can look through to find trends in occupations there over time.

If one wanted to explore Moravian communities in the country as a whole, here's another way to use the Master Search, by searching for 'Moravian' as a keyword search in the 1861 census. You can even bring up a map, which therefore shows where the Moravian faith was most concentrated. The site can also generate these maps from census or civil registration data for any surname.

Another key type of record useful for local history and available at the site are trade directories. There are hundreds of these available, and many of them provide information about specific places such as the basis of the local economy, topographical details and so on.

---

# RESEARCH TIPS

- Many CROs aren't spacious – book a study space.
- Check historic county boundaries – these may affect where archives are kept (resources such as www.genuki.org.uk can help, as well as the historic counties gazetteer at www.gazetteer.org.uk)
- Use censuses as a source: they can tell you a great deal about localities, for example, what kinds of workers lived there, or how many people lived under one roof.
- Find out if there are any museums, large houses, businesses and so on in your area of study that may retain their own records.
- The CARN (County Archive Research Network) scheme offers benefits for researchers: visit www.archives.org.uk.
- Forums such as www.rootschat.com can prove invaluable sources of advice and encouragement – register (for free) in order to participate.
- Also useful is the place-themed message board at www.curiousfox.com
- Explore many historical accounts of British places at www.british-history.ac.uk

---

information is available elsewhere.

Every county also has a CRO (sometimes called county archives). CRO holdings also vary, but will likely include primary, sources such as rate books, Quarter Sessions records, council minutes, archives of schools and photographs. Sometimes material will be on microfiche.

A quick web search reveals how many local history societies there are in Britain. It's certainly worth joining one: membership is cheap, and you will benefit from the knowledge and advice of other researchers. For example, say that your interests are focused on Northumberland. The umbrella Association of Northumberland Local History Societies (ANLHS) lists over 50 regional societies, from Berwick to Wylam.

There is no definitive directory of local history societies, but the largest list, with more than 1200 of them, can be found at **www.local-history.co.uk/Groups/index.html**.

### Online help

As well as enabling researchers to find out a great deal without ever leaving the comfort of home, the internet is full of other useful information for those new to local history pursuits. It's impossible to do much more that skim the online surface here, but the following websites will be helpful.

The British Association for Local History (**www.balh.co.uk**) was set up to encourage and help those studying local history academically or for leisure. As well as publishing a journal and local history magazine, it organises guided visits to places of interest and offers members various benefits, including reduced rates for local history events. Its website has an especially useful 'links' section that points users towards national regional societies and groups, local history courses and training, and publishers of useful books, guides, maps and other resources. Individual membership currently costs £30 a year.

The National Archives' (TNA) website contains a directory of other archives (**http://discovery.nationalarchives.gov.uk/find-an-archive**), in which users can find contact details for UK, Republic of Ireland, Channel Islands and Isle of Man record repositories. As TNA is the official records repository for the UK, its website is of immense use to local historians – the homepage (**www.nationalarchives.gov.uk**) includes links that will help with your research, and it's well worth browsing the site's contents. Those researching in Northern Ireland should also visit the Public Record Office of Northern Ireland website (**www.proni.gov.uk**) and for the Republic the National Archives of Ireland at **www.nationalarchives.ie**; for Scotland, check out **www.nas.gov.uk** and **www.scotlandspeoplehub.gov.uk**.

Another valuable resource (although not free) is the British Library Newspaper Archive (**www.britishnewspaperarchive.co.uk**). Scanned pages of countrywide historic newspapers can be filtered by date, county, region, place and newspaper title. Also worthy of mention is A Vision of Britain (**www.visionofbritain.org.uk**), which includes maps, statistical trends and historical descriptions of Britain from 1801–2001, and **www.archiveshub.ac.uk** may also prove useful in locating resources.

### How can local history inform family history research?

"Local history brings history home, it touches your life, the life of your family, your neighbourhood, your community." This succinct quotation from American historian Thomas Noel answers the question perfectly. If there's one thing family historians are seeking, it's a knowledge of our forebears, including where they lived, worked and played. After all, a deeper appreciation of who they were leads us to better understand who we are.

**JILL MORRIS** is an experienced copy editor and teacher and a part-time PhD student at Leeds University.

# Picturing the past

*Introducing a valuable online resource for bring the past to life*

F amily history data website **TheGenealogist.co.uk** has become the first family history website to launch a dedicated Image Archive that allows you to view historic images in both standard and '3D' forms. These historical pictures allow you to relive the past through the eyes of your ancestors. The standard images are free for everyone to search and view and cover the period from 1850 to 1940. You can explore thousands of images there – with more being added regularly – via **www.TheGenealogist.co.uk/ImageArchive**.

We all want to know more about the lives our ancestors led. Adding a picture to the family story is the perfect complement to any research. TheGenealogist's new Image Archive allows anyone to search and view images of towns, landmarks, churches, resorts, occupations and military campaigns. They also include images of social interest showing how your ancestors could have led their lives. You may even be able to find the church were your ancestor was baptised or married.

Diamond subscribers to TheGenealogist can also view and download

You can search by title and keywords or filter by category such as 'occupation' or 'building'

'3D' images can be viewed either as 'wigglegrams' (animated images flipping back and forth between two frames) or standard 'red and blue' image like the one at the right, which comes to life when you wear 3D glasses the images in a high resolution format for extra clarity.

The Image Archive is fully searchable and is divided up into sections to allow users to find relevant images of interest, quickly and easily. You can search by keyword or title. All the images are tagged and rated for quality to further assist the researcher.

Hundreds of the images are also available in stunning '3D' to really bring the past to life. With scenes of the hustle and bustle of market day to the drama of war, there's a selection to view as both 3D moving images and as 3D 'red blue' images (requiring tinted glasses).

Many other scenes are available in a standard format to view, with images not only from the British Isles but also internationally, with scenes ranging from Aldershot to Zanzibar. On these pages we showcase a variety of the images available and how they can illuminate the past.

**Right is Luton Salvation Army Band posed in someone's garden in 1890**

**Slices of social history: the picture to the left shows people dancing on Blackpool Pier in 1897. Below is one of many colour images in the collection, from a postcard depicting different scenes in a Lancashire cotton mill**

**Wartime also features in the image archive. Above are British Royal Engineers constructing second line trenches in Flanders in WW1**

# Jutland remembered

*Records from the largest naval battle of WW1 are online*

Did your ancestor participate in the largest naval battle of World War One? A full record set of the Royal Navy servicemen killed or wounded in the Battle of Jutland is available to Gold and Diamond subscribers at data website **TheGenealogist.co.uk**.

After a number of smaller naval engagements in the first two years of World War One, the Battle of Jutland was the first major naval battle involving large dreadnought battleships on both sides. Involving 250 ships and around 100,000 men it was also the major naval battle of the war.

After breaking German codes, the British knew of the German plan to try to destroy their fleet in two engagements; they left port to gain the element of surprise and catch the German fleet off the coast of Denmark. What was hoped to be a decisive British victory turned into a confused and bloody battle with many British casualties.

The Royal Navy lost 14 ships and suffered nearly 7,000 casualties. The Germans lost 11 ships and 2,551 men. Confused leadership and poor quality ammunition hindered the Royal Navy in the battle and the losses shook morale in Britain at the time.

The Battle of Jutland records provide a full list of the men killed or wounded in the battle with their rank, name of ship and date of death taken from official Admiralty sources. The Battle of Jutland Roll of Honour database was initially based upon the Admiralty's Registers of Killed and Wounded (in The National Archives record series ADM 104). These were cross-referenced with the Naval Who's Who of 1917 and subsequently the Commonwealth War Graves Commission and other TNA records. Where possible the records online are cross-referenced to entries at the CWGC's website, as with other Roll of Honour records at TheGenealogist.

Records of the men lost range from Rear Admiral Robert Arbuthnot, commander of the 1st Cruiser Squadron who went down with his flagship HMS Defence, to 16-year-old Jack Rutland who – although mortally wounded – stayed at his post on board the damaged HMS Chester. Although the losses were heavy, the Royal Navy was still a major fighting force and the German fleet never put to sea again in such large numbers to channel British sea superiority.

The records are available to view in the 'Roll of Honour' section of the Military Records at TheGenealogist.